SPECIAL MESSAGE FROM HEAVEN

"Go ye into all the world and preach the gospel to every creature. He who believes and is baptized will be saved; but he who does not believe will be condemned. And these signs will follow those who believe: In my name they will cast out demons; they will speak with new tongues; they will take up serpent; and if they drink anything deadly, it will by no means hurt them; they will lay hands on the sick, and they will recover".

Mark 16:15-18

All inquiries should be addressed to:

Book Domain LLC.
543 E Louise Dr Phoenix, Az 85050

Ordering Information:
Amount Deals. Special rebates are accessible on the amount bought by corporations, associations, and others. For points of interest, contact the distributor at the address above.

Cover by Julio Martinez

Printed in the United States of America.

ISBN-13   Paperback   978-1-967903-36-8
           eBook   978-1-967903-35-1

Library of Congress Control Number: 2025911694

SPECIAL MESSAGE FROM
HEAVEN

MARY ADERONKE
MORENIKE JAIYEOBA

BOOK DOMAIN LLC

This Book is dedicated to

The Father,
The Son
And
The
Holy Spirit

I dedicate this book to:

My grandmother, Mrs. Abigail Atinuke Jaiyeoba who taught me the way of the Lord and gave me her love and support throughout my childhood. Thank you for teaching me diligence and obedience to God in all my endeavor.

My Uncle Dr. K.T Jaiyeoba and His wife Dr. Bola Jaiyeoba. Thank you for everything you have done for me throughout my childhood. I thank you for your love and support, and for taking the role of my father and mother in my life. Thank you for your love and caring through prayers and guidance. May God reward you.

I want to thank God for my father, Michaael Jaiyeoba, for what he has done for me as well.

My sweet mother in the Lord Pastor Wapaemi Wariboko for being caring and for God to use you as a point of contact in my life. Thank you for giving me word of wisdom and understanding in knowing the will of God in my life. Thank you for all your provision and support. My Lord will supply all your needs according to His riches in glory by Christ Jesus.

My precious sister in the Lord, Sister Funmi Agbaje and her husband, for all their care and support in my children's life. Thank you for the Christ Our Foundation Learning Center for helping my children to grow in the Lord. You have done the best job a mother and father could do for their children. May God bless you all.

To: my daughter
Mary Aderonke Morenike Jaiyeoba
From: Jesus Christ

"My daughter, Aderonke, I knew you before you were born you were fearfully and wonderfully made. Your birth was not an accident, your Heavenly Father planned it. I created you to become a useful vessel in my hand. Your message to the world is to share the gospel of Jesus Christ so that people would repent of their sin and turn to God for Salvation in order for them to inherit the kingdom of God"

CONTENTS

1

MY FIRST TRIP TO HEAVEN
WITH TWO ANGELS

HAVE YOU EVER WONDERED THE GOD'S purpose for your life? Have you met with God? Has He spoken to you? Many at times, I had pondered on these questions. I wondered why God had to set me apart for his work. Then I remembered visiting my grandmother's uncle who was the founder of *Bishop Akinyele Church at Ibadan.* My grandmother's uncle was the first Archbishop of Ibadan in Nigeria. (Reverend A.B Akinyele while his brother, the Oba I.B Akinyele was the first Olubadan of Ibadan (the King) and they both did service for the Lord. I also have uncles who were also reverend in the church, and they all did service for the Lord as well. My grandmother knew from the time I was a child that the Lord had set me apart to become a vessel in His vineyard. I went out with my aunty for evangelism, and I learned to give out Christian tracts at a younger age. My grandmother taught me the word of God and prepared me to be useful in God's kingdom.

My story began on the night my grandmother called the family members for prayer. My grandmother's favorite hymn was "Now Thank We All Our God." We do our devotion in the morning, also at night and then we pray. I can never forget that night we all finished the prayer and went to bed, something mysterious happened to me. I saw a bright light that showed through the window. When the light moved toward my direction, I changed the position I slept because the light reflection disturbed me. Then the light moved toward the direction I changed to. Later I saw a stairway from Heaven that ended at my front door and Angels of God were descending from it. The two Angels came to my room and the moment they entered; fear overshadowed me. One of the Angels saw fear on my face and said, "We are messengers from God. I run errands for Jesus and the other angel is your Guidance Angel." The Guidance Angel said, "I have been with you from the time you were born till now. The Lord has sent us to you, and you must come with us." The moment, he said that I followed them, and we were ascending toward Heaven. **This was like Jacob's experience at Bethel.**

> "When he reached a certain place, he stopped for the night because it was sunset. Taking one of the stones there, he put it under his head, and he lay down to sleep. He dreamt, in which he saw stairway resting on earth with its top reaching the Heaven and Angels of God were ascending and descending on it"

> (Genesis 28:11-12).

INSIDE HEAVEN

When we got to a stop, I found myself in a glorious place and my eyes could not behold it. The Angels who brought me looked at me, smiled and one of them said, "This is Heaven, the Throne of God." I had voices singing and shouting Halleluiah, but did not see anyone. We began to walk until we reached a place where I saw thousands of people in bright white linen and I discovered that they did not have wings like Angels, and they looked like me. The Angel told me that the people I saw singing praises and Halleluiah to the King of Kings and Lord of Lords were Saints. The Saints had been washed by the Blood of the Lamb and were waiting for the coming of Our Lord Jesus Christ. As we continued our journey, I saw a building that was so majestic that I never saw a building like that on earth. The structure of the building was made of gold and it did not need light because the glory of God showed through it. As we went further, I could hear other voices singing and the more we got closer, the more I heard the music. When we got to the part of the building, I asked the Angels that took me to Heaven about those who were singing praises to the Almighty God. The Angel replied, "My child, these flowers you see were the ones singing day and night because they were waiting for the coming of the saints". We continued to walk further until we reached the Throne of God and as we got there, I saw 24 elders seating around the Throne of God with their white bright cloth. Their attire was so different that it was glistening through my eyes, and they had on their heads the crown of gold with 12 stars around it. These twenty-four elders worshipped God day and night by bowing down to His Throne. At a certain point we stopped, and we cannot go further, until I heard sound of trumpet and instrument playing. The Angels of God were the one playing the instrument to worship the Kings of Kings and Lords of Lord. I had the Host of Heaven worship the Lamb and bowed down to His Throne. The saints who were being washed by the Blood of the Lamb also worshipped Him, the One who sat on the Throne. I heard the host of Heaven worship the Lamb and bowed down to the Throne after the trumpet sound. I saw myself bowed down to the Throne of God as well. Later, I heard footsteps coming toward my direction but did not see anyone. I felt someone touching my hand and the voice said, "I am Jesus Christ". When I looked up, my eyes could not behold him because the blood was gushing down His face. He took me by hand and said, "My child you must prepare my people for the kingdom of God. You must write down what you see and hear. Tell my people to accept me as their personal Lord and Savior. Let them know that I Jesus Christ came to the world and die for their sin. Let them know that Heaven and Hell is real. Go my daughter proclaim the good news to my people that I am coming soon". After the Lord had spoken, I got up and the Angel escort me out and we were both descending back to the earth where I found myself back on my bed. That morning when I woke up, I ran outside of the house to see if the stairs was still there but when I looked, I saw nothing. I now discovered that it was a vision. I did not expect that the Lord would set me apart for His work. I began to wonder why? Among all my family, Lord singles me out for His work. At that tender age, I did not expect that I would become a pastor or evangelist in one day. When Lord told me that He had chosen me to be a vessel in His vineyard, I had no objection to that.

I was raised in a Christian home where I spent most of my time with my great grand uncle, the founder of Bishop Akinyele. I watched and learned from him. I did not know that he was training me to be a vessel in God's kingdom. I then understood when the Lord told me that I had been chosen to be a vessel in His hand. The next morning, I told my grandmother about my encounter with the Lord. My grandmother smiled and said she knew from the time I was born that I was going to be great in life and that there was a place that the Lord was taking me. My grandmother also spoke to me and said, "My granddaughter, Lord had a reason for choosing you because you had a special gift that the Lord had instilled in you. I would do my part to train you the way of the Lord and you also had to do your part as well".

2

REVELATION OF HEAVEN

IN HEAVEN, GOD IS OMNIPRESENT, AND He is present everywhere at the same time. Our God observes everything that we do. God is different and independent from His creation. Our God is Eternal-He is from everlasting to everlasting (Ps. 90:1-2). There is no change in God's attributes in perfection or in His purpose for mankind. He is perfect and holy and completely without blemish or sin and He is righteous. The Lord revealed to me the City of Jerusalem, the city was so significant in the beginning of the church. Jerusalem was the birthplace of Christianity. It was there that Jesus was crucified and rose from the dead. It was also in Jerusalem that exalted Christ poured out the Holy Spirit on His disciples at Pentecost (Act 2). From that city, gospel message of Jesus Christ started and spread unto the uttermost part of the earth (Act 1:8). Instead of preparing a city on the earth for believers, God is busy preparing the "New Jerusalem", which will someday become the ruling place of Jesus who will come down from God, out of Heaven as a prepared bride adorned for her husband (Rev.21:2). On that great day, God's covenant promise will be fully realized: "Behold the tabernacle of God with men, and He will dwell with them, and they shall be His people and God Himself shall be with them and be their God" (Rev 21:3). God and Lamb will reign forever and ever on their throne in the Holy City (Rev 22:3-5). Many believe that when Christ returns to establish His millennial rule (Rev 20:1-6), He will set up His throne in the city of Jerusalem after the Great White Throne Judgment (Rev 20:1-5), the Heavenly Jerusalem will descend to the new earth and become the Headquarters of God's Eternal Kingdom (Rev 21:2).

REVELATION OF HELL

After seeing the Revelation of Heaven, I was taken to another building. I saw an Angel stretch his hand and the gate opened the moment we entered the building. The Gate was the **Gate of Hell** and the moment the gate opened, I heard people crying and screaming and cursing themselves for being in such a horrible place. The rate at which the fire in hell burned was unbearable. When I moved closer to the Gate of Hell, the people seemed to be aware of my presence but did not see an Angel who was with me. I could hear what the people were saying. They cried for water to drink because they were thirsty, and some screamed that the fire was hot and burning them. The people in Hell fire had bodies like us but their souls were burning in Hell. The more I got closer, the more they seemed to be aware of my presence, and one of them was screaming, "Please help me. I was a pastor of a church. I did not forgive my fellow pastor for what he did to me". I was heading toward the pastor when an Angel pulled me back and said, "You cannot go there!". I was told by the Lord to show you so that you will warn His people to repent and come to Him. All those who committed murder, unforgiveness, backbiting, gossiper, fornicator, adulterer, drunkenness, and stealing all ended up in Hell Fire. Their souls were burning in Hell because they had turned their back from God.

There were two walls in the building, one was dark, and the other was red. In that building, I saw some people eating their own flesh and I asked the Angel who came with me why those people were eating their own flesh. The angel replied that those people were the ones eating other people's flesh when they were on earth. Many of those who did not accept Jesus as their Lord and Savior were in Hell Fire. There was no mercy in Hell Fire. The demons in hell would pierce a fork-like into the person's stomach. The demons would use their sharp claws to pull out their hair and the teeth of the flesh eaters out and would torment them day and night. I got so scared when I saw the number of people the devil had tormented. The souls of the people under tormentor were burning in Hell because they had turned away from God. Many Christians, deacons, deaconesses, general overseers, bishops, pastors, elders, and unbelievers had their part in Hell Fire.

Where do you want to spend your eternity? Choose where you want to spend the rest of your life today. Hell is real, so is Heaven. Repent and give your life to Christ and stay away from sin.

3

MESSAGE FROM THE LORD JESUS CHRIST

IN A BUILDING, I SAW PEOPLE crying for salvation and screaming that the Lord should save them from devil's torment and at that moment, I began to pray to God to save the people's souls. As I was praying, my eyes were wide opened, and I saw Christ Himself with seven candles in His hands. Lord Jesus said, "My child, these seven candles you see in my hand represent seven churches on earth that would be judged by me according to their deeds. Among these seven churches, three gave the devil foothold in their lives and if they did not turn back and return to me, I would punish them. You have been chosen to proclaim the good news to the people so that they can turn from their evil way and follow my path of righteousness." The moment the Lord spoke, I found myself in the church. In that church, a one-year-old boy cried furiously, and his grandmother could not control him. As I was pacing around to see what would become of that boy, I had a voice behind me saying, "You had no right to be here." The moment he said that I saw a huge Angel with a bowl full of wrath upon the man who said you had no right to be here. The man screamed to death. Within a second, I saw another two Angels with the Ark of God and the whole place was in disarray when the people saw the ark. The devil and his demons were bound and thrown in the fire and that was how the Lord won the battle. Later that day, Lord Jesus spoke, "MY DAUGHTER, ADERONKE, I CREATED YOU AND I KNEW YOU BEFORE I FORMED YOU IN YOUR MOTHER'S WOMB. YOU WERE FEARFULLY AND WONDERFULLY MADE. DEAR CHILD, THROUGH MY SPIRIT YOU RECEIVE GUIDANCE BEYOND THE KNOWLEDGE OF THIS WORLD. EACH TIME YOU LISTEN TO MY VOICE YOU BECOME CLOSER TO YOUR DREAMS. ALL HAS BEEN A SEASON OF TRAINING AND TEACHING THAT YOU HAVE ENDURED THESE PAST TIMES. YOU HAVE ENDURED SUPPRESSION, REPRESSION AND EVEN DEPRESSION. BUT I SAY TO YOU THAT ALL OF THESE SHALL BE TURNED INTO A TIME OF GLORIOUS EXPRESSION. INDEED, I HAVE PREPARED FOR YOU A TABLE ABUNDANT WITH GOOD THINGS FOR YOU. REMEMBER THAT YOU CAN NEVER GO BEYOND MY LOVE AND CARE. FOR I AM THE LORD WHO LOVES YOU, AND I NEVER STOP LOVING YOU. EVEN WHEN YOU MAKE MISTAKES AND GO THE WRONG WAY, I AM STILL THERE. I WILL ALWAYS LOVE YOU, MY CHILD AND NOTHING CAN CHANGE THIS. ALWAYS BE READY FOR THE MANIFESTATION OF MY WORK."

MY GRANDMOTHER'S MESSAGE

The following morning when I woke up, I told my grandmother about my encounter with Lord Jesus Christ. My grandmother looked at me and smiled. She said, "The Lord Jesus called you to be a vessel in His hand. Obedience to God is better than a sacrifice. Follow His footsteps and He will direct your part. My granddaughter never departed from the way of the Lord; allow Him to use you and make sure you keep His commandment." Later that evening, I went to bed as usual. Then at midnight, someone called my name, I woke up. I went to my grandmother, and I told her someone called my name. The experience reoccurred three times. My grandmother told me to say, "Speak Lord, your servant is listening". I said the statement when I went back to bed, and that was my second encounter with the Lord. Since then, Lord Jesus began to communicate with me and told me what He wanted me to do. I told my grandmother when I woke up that God spoke to me, that He had chosen me as a vessel for His kingdom. My grandmother said, "Did you understand what God meant? It meant that God had set you apart to be a worker in His vineyard. I believe in my heart that Lord will teach you what to do when the time comes. You, my granddaughter need to follow His direction and He will direct your path because you were not just an ordinary child". She said further that God had chosen me to be a vessel in His hand. Then my grandmother read the story of a boy named Samuel in (1 Samuel 3:1-10). God called Samuel when he was in the temple with Eli. God ministered to him and told him he would become a leader in Israel. Later that morning, my grandmother gave me her last admonition on my spiritual encounter with a bible passage - "Keep God's commandment with this bible passage: Proverb 3: 1-6. "My child forgets not my law but let thine heart keep my commandment: for length of days and long life, and peace shall they add to thee. Let not mercy and truth forsake thee: bind them about thy neck; write them upon the tablet of thine heart: so shalt thou find favor and good understanding in the sight of God and man. Trust in the Lord with all thine heart and lean not unto thine own understanding. In all thine ways acknowledge him, and he shall direct thy paths." Remember you were a gift from God, and He is ready to use you for his own purpose.

4

A WOMAN WHO GOT SAVED

FIVE YEARS AFTER I RELOCATED TO United States of America, I got a college admission. I was doing well in all my classes because the Lord was there with me. During my third semester in college, I joined the United Christian fellowship. I taught bible study and prayed along with those students who have a prayer requests. I did not know that the hand of God was heavy upon me at that time. The Lord answered the prayer of those students I got in contact with and whenever I had a break in between my classes, I always go to the library to study and some of the students would come to me and tell me that they wanted to learn more about Jesus. I spent my leisure time teaching them the word of God and some of them gave their lives to Christ. It was during a prayer time that I met one of my classmates who had a tough time at home. Her mother was not saved because she practiced voodoo at home. So, we believers gathered together to intercede for her mother. When I got home later that evening, I prayed as usual and went to bed. Around 3AM, the Lord woke me up and I began to pray concerning my classmate's mother. As I was praying, I saw in the spirit that I was in the woman's house praying and biding the spirit that did not represent God's image in her house. As we were praying, her mother came out and told us that if we did not leave her house, she would call the police on us. My classmate just told us to leave because her mother meant business. So, we went outside the house, and we prayed again. The prayer point for that night was **"Any power that did not represent God's image in this house should catch fire."** As we were praying, I heard a screamed inside the house, and we all ran inside. When we got there, we saw the mother of this woman lying on the floor, screaming that fire was burning her body. Then I asked her if she was ready to give her life to Christ and she answered that she was ready. I asked the mother of this woman to repeat a word after me; **"Heavenly Father, I come in the name of Jesus Christ. I believe in my heart that Jesus Christ is the Son of God. I believe in my heart that He died for my sins, I believe that you raise Him from the dead for my Justification. I receive Him today as my personal Lord and Savior and I give God the Glory. Amen."** After she said the confession, the vision disappeared. When I got to school the following day, I asked one of my friends about the lady who came to United Christian fellowship, and she told me she never saw her. For two weeks, I did not see this lady and on the third week, I heard someone call out my name on my way to the library. When I looked back, I saw the same lady I prayed for in that vision. She ran toward me so excited and told me that she had been preparing for her wedding with her mother. She told me that her mother gave her life to Christ. When I asked, when did her mother gave her life to Christ, she said it was two weeks ago and I was surprised because it was the same time I and my fellow workers in the Christian fellowship prayed for her. That was how Lord Jesus saved her mother.

Later that afternoon, I realized that the hand of the Lord was heavy upon me. God was always there with me and answered my prayer when I called upon Him. Sometimes when I prayed on behalf of my friends and brought their case to the Lord, the Lord is always answering their prayer. Sometimes I found myself praying in the spirit, the prayer always comes to reality. My friends always come back to tell me that their prayers had been answered. I was in the library one day, after my encounter with Lord Jesus when one of my friend came to see me. When she saw me, she said, "Ronke, your face was radiant it looked like you had seen Jesus". I got up and told my friend that I would be back, and I quickly ran to the bathroom and looked at the mirror to see what my friend was talking about, but I did not see anything. My friend could see the glory of God in my life and the radiant of the Lord was upon me and that was like what children of Israel saw on Moses when he came down from the Mountain.

When Moses came down from Mount Sinai with the two tablets of the covenant law in his hands, he was not aware that his face was radiant because he had spoken with the Lord. When Aaron and all the Israelites saw Moses, his face was radiant, and they were afraid to come near him. But Moses called to them; so, Aaron and all the leaders of the community came back to him, and he spoke to them. Afterward all the Israelites came near him, and he gave them all the commands the Lord had given him on Mount Sinai. When Moses finished speaking to them, he put a veil over his face. But whenever he entered the Lord's presence to speak with him, he removed the veil until he came out. And when he came and told the Israelites what he had been commanded, they saw that his face was radiant. Then Moses would put the veil back over his face until he went back to speak with the Lord.

Exodus 34:29-35.

When I got home that same day, the woman my father called my mother also said, "Ronke your face looks radiant", like my friend told me in school. I told her that my face was radiant because of the cream I applied on my face. She now insisted that I should give her same cream I used, and I did. Then on the following day, when I came back from school, she asked me the same question why my face was radiant because she applied the same cream I gave her, but nothing happened. The woman said, "You this girl did not tell me why your face was radiant", and I was not happy at the moment because I did not understand why she kept on asking me same question over and over after given her the cream to apply on her face. Then I heard a voice clearly telling me don't be angry, why not respond to the question she asked. Then at that moment I knew that voice was the voice of Jesus. When she asked me the same question the third day I was about to go to school, she approached me and said "you this girl did not tell me why your face was shining, and I replied that it was Jesus that make my face to shine. The moment I said the word Jesus she slapped my face and tears fell from my eyes. I knew from that day she was not happy about my relationship with God. Throughout my entire life as a young teenage girl, Lord was always there with me and never left me alone. God was always sending His Holy Spirit to teach me His word.

5

SECOND TRIP TO HEAVEN

I WAS UPON MY BED ONE night, when I saw two Angels of God in my room. I became frighten when I saw them. One of them looked at me and said, "Do not be afraid we were sent by Jesus. I ran errand for Jesus and He always sent me to minister to His children". The other Angel said, "I was there the day you were born till now. You must come with us because the Lord had a mission for you to attend". I was lifted in the spirit and were going back to Heaven. We were ascending back to Heaven through a ladder that almost reached the Throne of God. As we got to Heaven, the Angel at the gate did not let me enter. He said we had to sing along with those who praised and worshipped God before we can enter. There was 12 Pearl Gates, and we can only enter through one of them. As we got to the gate, the Angel who brought me told me to sing along with them and that was the only way I would be able to enter. I was engrossed with the music, and I began to sing along with them. Then the moment we began to sing, the gate opened, and we entered. This is the place where God lives, the House of God. The Angels worshipped God day and night with their trumpets and singing "Holy, Holy, Holy is the Lord. Blessed is He who comes in the name of the Lord".

> And again, they shouted: Halleluiah! The smoke from her goes up forever and ever. The twenty-four elders and their four creatures fell down and worshipped God who is seated on the throne and they cried: Halleluiah! Amen

> (Rev 19:3-5)

I saw the hosts of Heaven and each of them were unique in God's eyes. Some of these Angels had wings and others did not but they looked like one of us. As I looked, a diamond door opened, and someone came out and His appearance looked like the Son of man. The man approached us, and his face looked so different that I cannot behold Him with my eyes. His appearance looked like a bridegroom coming out of His chamber. Then I heard a voice like many waters, then there was a tiny voice and I could hear it clearly. The voice said, "Welcome to Heaven my precious daughter I am Jesus Christ".

PURIFICATION FROM THE LORD

I saw a purple gold book in His hand and my name was written on it. **Aderonke Morenike Jaiyeoba**. The book contained the history of my life from the time I was born till now. Lord looked at me for sometime and said to the Angel "purified this child and bring her back to me." There was a mission for us to attend. The moment the

Lord had spoken, my guardian angel took me away and we went outside the Heaven. We walked down through the beautiful gate and a diamond door opened. We entered a room, and it was full of water, living water as described in the Book of Revelation.

> Then the angel showed me a river with water of life, clear like crystal flowing from the Throne of God and of the Lamb. It flowed down the Center of the Main Street.
>
> (Rev. 22:1-2).

The angel told me to get inside the water and dip me through it from head to toe. When I came out of the water, I looked like one of the Angels. The Angel put on the white garment on me, and we went through another gate. The moment the gate opened we entered, and I could smell the scent of nature. The Angel used the oil on me according to the word of the Lord. The Angel took me back to where the Lord was and I found myself at the Throne of God. Lord took my hand and said, "my child come with me" and we were between the Heaven and earth, when I found myself in a small town.

6

MISSION FROM THE LORD JESUS CHRIST

THAT MORNING, I SAW MYSELF DRIVING a red car toward that small city and the moment I turned to the right corner, I saw a signed post, and **Welcome to Western Shore** was written on it. I came out of the car, and I looked around the area of where God wanted me to minister. Later I asked people in that area about the Western Shore Church, and I was given directions to the church. As I was coming out of the car a man and a woman approached me and welcome me to their town. Then they took me to a motel room where I would be staying for the crusade. That evening at the motel room, I prayed to God for journey mercy and the Lord will give me an utterance to speak to His people. As I was praying, I felt the presence of the Lord in the room, and I could hear His voice that evening He came. The Lord came to me and said my child get up and follow me, and I found myself stood up and followed Him until we reached the front of the building. The Lord told me that the town needed deliverance and I had been chosen as a vessel to deliver them from the hand of the oppressor. Lord spoke again, "my child you must bring good news to this town so that my people would repent. Now prepare yourself for the mission I will send you." "You must prepare my people for the kingdom of God." The moment Lord Jesus said that, I found myself in the church.

SERVICE IN THE CHURCH

When I got inside the church, the service already started. The choirs started the praise and worship songs. I saw the multitude of people worshipped and praise God in their language. In the mixed of worshipped, Lord said, "my child come along with me", and we began to walk toward the pulpit and Lord told me to sit down. The moment we sat down I saw the hymn songs for that morning. The hymn song was, "What a Friend we have in Jesus." As the choir sang, then I noticed the men in white bright robe at the right corner of the church. The angels were so unique and beautiful, and their attire looked different. These were the ministering angels. They ministered in songs with their trumpets. It was so marvelous how they worshipped God on the throne. I thought the people around me were aware of these angels, but they were not, except me. I asked the Lord Jesus who were this spirit being in the white robe attire, and the Lord replied to me, these were ministering angels.

> Are not all angels ministering spirits sent to serve those who will inherit salvation?
>
> Hebrew 1:14

Go now to the pulpit and ministered to my people. I thank God for giving me an opportunity to speak to His people. My main topic for the sermon was **"What Must I Do to Be Saved."** The reading was taken from John 3:16-17. To be saved meant to deliver from sin or preserve salvation. God wanted to have a personal relationship with you. John 17:3 and this is the way to have eternal life to know you, the Only One true God and Jesus Christ, the One you sent to earth. God was not some force unspeaking or unseeing idol or merely another name for your own self-esteem. Instead, God was a person, your creator, who created you to be in relationship with Him. Why? Because you can turn your life over to God's control because He loves what was best for you. In fact, He loves you so much that He gave His Son, Jesus to die on the cross for you. When you turn your life to Him, you are given your life to the One who know you inside out.

> For God so loved the world so much that He gave His Only Son, so that everyone who believes in Him will not perish but have eternal life. For God did not send His Son into the world to condemn the world, but that the world through Him might be saved

> (John 3:16-17)

Remember that Jesus died to take the penalty for the sins we deserved. He took our punishment that we would not have to! Jesus, the way was prepared for us to be able to have personal relationship with the Holy God. You must personally respond by trusting Jesus as your Lord and Savior. The book of Romans said.

> If we confess with your mouth that Jesus is Lord and believe in your heart that God raised Him

from the dead, you will be saved. For it is by believing in your heart that you are made right with God, and it is by confession with your mouth that you are saved.

(Roman 10:9-10)

You simply need to believe and receive Christ means acknowledging your belief in Christ, invite Him to come into your life, turning to God from present way of living (repentance) and beginning the adventure of directing your life. After the sermon, I asked the people that would give their life to Christ to come out. I told them to repeat a word after me. This was the word. "Dear God, I know that my sin has separated me from you. Thank you that Jesus died in my place. I asked Jesus to forgive my sin and to come into my life. I renounce the devil. Please begin to direct my life and thank you for giving me eternal life. In Jesus' name I pray Amen." After the short prayer, the choir sang, **I Surrender All.** As they were singing, something mysterious happened and I noticed those spiritual being and I thought to myself, how was it possible to see them but God made it possible. I saw this spiritual being and they were also called an angel of God. As I was watching, I noticed that one of the angels of God, had a Scroll Book in his hand and he wrote down the name of those who gave their life to Christ. I could see in the scroll, that he wrote the person's name, date of birth, the month, the day, the time, the minutes, the second and the place the person gave his or her life to Christ. In another session, I saw ministering angels; they were ministered to those who gave their lives to Christ. In that vision, many people were saved that day.

Are not all angels ministering spirits, sent forth to
minister for them who shall be heirs of salvation?

(Hebrew 1:14)

After the vision Lord gave me, I went out for evangelism. I
bought the New Testament Bible and distributed it to people while
doing the evangelism. I spoke to different people with different language about Christ and many gave their lives to Christ. While doing
my ministration outside, I met a Spanish woman while doing an
evangelism, I gave her a New Testament English Bible, and she told
me she did not understand English. So, she requested for Spanish
bible, and I gave her the New Testament Spanish Bible and she was
so excited and thank me. As I went further with my evangelism. I
met an elderly woman and ministered to her. After given her the
New Testament Bible, she said to me, "do you take donation", and
I replied, "no I don't accept donation because the salvation is free".
She smiled and said, "thank you for the New Testament Bible that
you gave me".

7

A DEMON POSSESSED WOMAN

Two months after the ministration, Lord Jesus took me to a room. In that room, I saw a woman lying down on the floor, and she looked very strange. Lord Jesus said, "Ronke, my daughter I had given you an authority to trample upon serpent and scorpion, over devil and his demon. You see my child, this woman had been possessed by the devil and you had been given a power from above to cast the demon out of her."

> And these signs shall follow them that believes; in my name shall they cast out devils and they shall speak with new tongues; they shall take up serpents; and if they drink any deadly things, it shall not hurt them, they shall lay hands on the sick, and they shall recover.
>
> Mark 16:17-18

Lord spoke to me again and said the story of this woman began the moment her mother stops her from going to church. She did not allow the woman to read her bible and pray in the house. The woman changed the moment she entered college and joined cult group in the school. She was influenced by one of her classmates who promised to protect her in time of trouble. Since her mother did not allow her to serve God, she decided to join them. Later the woman got sick, and the doctor cannot diagnose her sickness. She was later brought to the church by one of her friends. Now, her mother regrets what she did and wanted her daughter to be delivered. The Lord said," Aderonke my daughter, I had given you an authority to cast demon out of her". Later I found myself praying in spirit seeking the Lord's guidance in this area of deliverance. As I was praying, I found myself in a big building, in that building, I saw myself went down the stairs until I met a half human, half fish by the door. That mermaid did not allow me to enter. She said you had no right to be here. When I said, I bind you in the name of Jesus, the building shook and she said, do not mention the name of Jesus here again. As I came downstairs, I saw a lot of people being tied down and screaming for their lives. They had been tied down by the devil and his demon. It was in this building that I met the young woman that the Lord Jesus talked about. As I began to pray, they also began to wage war against me, but the Lord's power was stronger than their own. When I called fire of Holy Ghost to consume all power of darkness, then I heard an enraged voice shouted angrily and said, "you cannot stop us we were going to destroy this place". Then I heard another voice that said, "my child I had not given you the spirit of fear". Put on your whole Armor of God and you would overcome. The Lord revealed to me that the voice that I heard was the head of the demon and his name was Najid. He was put in charge of these people that were possessed. He controlled their mind and soul. Then, I said it was written, that every knee must bow, and every tongue must confess that Jesus Christ is the Lord. I soaked this house in the Blood of Jesus and covered with Holy Ghost Fire. The moment I entered the room, the demon in her spoke and said, leave us alone what do you want with us and we had nothing to do with you. I saw that the Spirit God was upon me and with violent spirit I commanded the demon to be quiet in the name of Jesus. I said:

> "But thus, say the Lord, even the captives of the might shall be taken away, and the prey of the terrible shall be delivered for I will contend with him that contends with thee, and I will save thy children." I will feed them that oppress thee with their own flesh: and they shall be drunk with their own blood, as with sweet wine and all flesh shall know that I Lord am thy Savior and Redeemer, the mighty One of Jacob."

> (Isaiah 49:25-26).

> "No weapon that is formed against thee shall prosper and every tongue that shall rise against thee in judgment thou shall condemn. This is the heritage of the servants of the Lord and righteousness is of me, says the Lord

> (Isaiah 54:17).

I said to the woman, the Lord declared, and I decreed that thou had been delivered in the hand of violent men. The moment

I said that the woman was delivered, and immediately I heard the voice of the Lord Jesus saying well done my precious daughter you had done well. The moment the Lord said that I woke up. The following day I went out for evangelism, and I met a young woman at the train station (subway). While I was given out the tract to the people on subway station, she was also doing the same thing as well. I talked to her, and asked her how long has she been going out to do evangelism, and she said not quiet long. We talked for a long time, she told me the story of her life and how she ended being a Satan's bride. She went for a deliverance, but nothing happened. She then asked me about any church where she can go to for a total deliverance, and I encourage her to go to Mountain of Fire. While I was still talking to that woman, the voice of the Lord interrupt our conversation and I heard the voice of the Lord telling me to pray along with her. We exchanged phone numbers, and I left subway station. At midnight my phone rang, and it happened to be that woman. I asked her what happened, and she said that she is under spiritual attacked and could not sleep. She stated that she sees demons in her room every night. I reminded her again that she still needed to go for deliverance, and she asked me if I knew any church that conducted such deliverance, and I replied to her about Mountain of Fire, and she told me that it was too far from where she lived. While she was still talking to me, I heard the voice of the Lord speaking to my spirit and said, my child why can't you take time to pray with her. I was hesitating to even go into warfare with this woman. I said, Lord you know this woman was once a Satan's Bride and her problem was beyond me. Lord spoke to me again and said my child, remember you are also the bride of Christ and the power to cast out has been given to you by me, and you had to use it ceaselessly. Since that night, I pray along with her every night. I brought her case to the Lord in prayer and in agreement we prayed together, and she was able to sleep. That woman I met at the subway station was the same woman Lord revealed to me in that vision.

Then two weeks after, I also began to face spiritual battle. The problem began after I finished prayer with this young woman, and I went to bed. I did not know what happened when I began to see demons in my room, and they looked like troll. My spiritual eyes were opened, and I could see them. They attacked me because I pray the deliverance prayer for the woman they had put in bondage. I was so weak that I could not move my body and one of my daughters woke up frightened because she saw a figure moving around the room and could not sleep. I had to pray with her and covered her with blood of Jesus and fire of the Holy Ghost, and went back to bed. The demons were not happy that I prayed with that young woman and they began to fight back. When I could not take the pain anymore, I cried to the Lord. I was so weak and tired when I saw two angelic beings in my room. One of the Angels said he ran errand for Jesus, and they were his messenger. Each time one of His children were in trouble, they were there to help. One of Angel carried me, and he was going toward the cloud until he reached a beautiful place that looked like a mansion. My eyes could not behold it because the whole place was made of gold. As we got there, we came to a room. In that room, Lord Jesus was waiting in His glorious appearance with white robe, and his face was radiant with full of light, and my eyes could not behold it. He sat down in a seat made of gold and Heaven was so beautiful, nothing can be compared with it. Lord took me from the angel and dip me in a water. The moment, the water was bubbling up, I could feel the healing process taken place. I cried the moment I felt the pain, and the Lord said my child, no tears in Heaven. Lord took the white cloth in His hand and wiped my face. I felt pain each moment the Lord touched my wound. Lord looked at me and said, "My child, you are not part of me if you did not let me heal your wound". Let me heal your wound so that you can get well. Every night, I felt the presence of the Lord in His glorious appearance in my room. I discovered that around 3am, the Lord would appear in a form of light and stayed with me. I began to learn new things from the Lord. After some time, Lord Jesus began to teach me how to become a prayer warrior. In a case scenario when the enemies began to attack, Lord Jesus said, "My child, you need to put on your whole Armor of God, the Breastplate and Shield of faith to confront the enemies. When the enemies rage and you think the battle is too much to bear, call upon me for the battle is mine". After the prayer, Lord Jesus turned to me and said, "MY DEAR ADERONKE, LOOK BEYOND THE PRESENT TRIALS AND TROUBLES, AND YOU WILL SEE THE PURPOSE AND PLAN TO WHICH ALL OF THIS IS LEADING. EACH STEP YOU MAKE IS TAKING YOU TO A MOUNTAIN TOP FROM WHICH MY GLORY WILL OPEN BEFORE YOU. DO NOT GROW TENSE AND DO NOT ALLOW FEAR TO DESTROY THE WORK I AM DOING. ALL IS FOR THE BEST. DO NOT FEAR THE CHANGES THAT ARE HAPPENING FOR I AM WITH YOU. TRUST ME BUT KNOW THAT I WILL DO THE BEST FOR YOU, FOR I AM THE LORD WHO CHANGES NOT. I SHALL LEAD YOU FROM THE VALLEY TO THE HEIGHTS OF JOY. MY CHILD ADERONKE, I AM TEACHING YOU SPIRITUAL POISE AND SOUL-BALANCING IN A VACILLATING, CHANGING WORLD. THE SAME POWER THAT CASTS OUT DEVILS IS YOURS. YOU MUST LEARN TO USE IT AND USE IT CEASELESSLY. I AM RELEASING MY JOY TO YOU. JOY THAT GIVES POWER TO DO ALL THAT YOU CAN ASK OR THINK, LIVE IN IT, BATHE IN IT. THE DAILY OBEYING OF MY SPIRITUAL DIRECTION WILL CREATE ALL THAT YOU

SEEK, DESIRE, AND CREATE THE SPIRITUAL HARMONY AND BEAUTY OF ALL THAT YOU ARE SEEKING TO HAVE IN YOUR LIFE. I AM YOUR WAY, AND I AM YOUR FATHER WHO LOVES YOU WITH ENDLESS LOVE." And that was the Lord's message to me.

8

VISITATION FROM THE LORD JESUS CHRIST

THE NIGHT OF JULY 1998, I just finished my prayer and bible reading when I saw a bright light shone through my window. The light was so bright that I could not behold it anymore. I was almost blind to see the light moving toward my direction. I first thought that it was the moonlight, but it was not. Later I saw a man in a white bright robe. His glorious appearance was so different my eyes could not behold him. Then I heard a voice from Heaven that said, "My child, prepare yourself and follow me. I Immediately got up and I followed him. Then I asked who you and He are replied I am Jesus Christ who came to the world to die for your sin, and I am the one who rose from the dead on the third day so that you can spend eternity with me. As He spoke, I followed Him, and we came to a certain point. The moment we got there, I saw a huge Angel who stood at the pole, His appearance was very radiant. He wore a bright white cloth that almost touched the floor. Everything in Heaven was gold and radiant. The Angel did not move from where he was, and his appearance was radiant from head to toe. My eyes could not behold him anymore. As we approached Heaven, there was a big wall made of gold. The wall was very tall and had no handle to open it. As we approached that big wall, we entered the room. In that room, there were bottles, some looked like clear glass and other looked like crystal. The bottle was plague with name on it. Inside the room I saw a man in a purple deep velvet robe. The robe was very beautiful. In the room was a table full of books lying on the table, some have diamond, pearls, and all of them were so amazing to the eyes. As Angel talked, another huge angel came through the door. He wore white glistening garment with gold-edge trim down in front of it. He was about twelve feet tall, and he had a bowl full of tears. The angel collected tears and put the tears in the bottles.

> "Now when He had taken the scroll, the four living creatures and the twenty-four elders fell down before the lamb each having a harp, and golden bowls full of incense, which are the prayers of the saints
>
> (Rev 5:8).

The name on the paper and bowl was given to the angel. Then the angel went to the room, read the note, and went to the place where bottle was kept, and he read the plague under the bottle. The angel then matched the name on the note with the bottle. Each time the saints cried to God and tears drop on the first page of the book, beautiful word began to appear to encourage them.

> "Your number my wandering; put my tears into your bottle; are they not in your book?
>
> (Ps 56:8).

33

After we left the room, we passed where beautiful white horses lived. The horses looked like marble chess pieces and they looked like huge statues. A woman dressed in a beautiful robe directed the horses to bow down before God's Throne.

> "Now I saw Heaven opened and behold a white horse. And He who sat on him was called Faithful and True and in Righteousness He judges and makes war. His eyes were like flame of fire, and on His head were many crowns. He had a name written that no one knew except Himself. He was clothed with a robe dipped in blood and His name is called The Word of God. And the armies in Heaven clothe in fine linen, white and clean, followed Him on white horses.
>
> (Rev 19:11-14).

One hour later, I was accompanied by an angel, and I heard a voice of the Lord, purified this child, and bring her back to me. The angel took me back to the room where the river flown over and as the angel deep me in the river, the river shouted Halleluiah. The moment that I came out of the water, my appearance changes to the glorious one and I was clothe in white garment. The angel took me back to where Lord Jesus was waiting for us. I saw the hosts of Heaven and each of them were unique in God's eyes. Some of these angels had wings and others did not; they looked like one of us.

Who are these angels that stood so radiant in a white robe and looked toward the radiant light the shone through Heaven? Then the angel replied that those were saints singing and shouting Halleluiah to the Lord and they were waiting for the coming of the Lord. We continued to move toward the direction I came from. The moment we got there; the angel left. I did not see the angel anymore. Then the Lord appeared in His radiant cloth and said, "My child, there is a mission for both of us to attend and I found myself in a room. In that room, many people were tied down and both their hands and legs were being tied to their bodies. "What have these people done? I asked the Lord. Then Lord replied, "My child these people you see had been tormented day and night by the devil and his demon and the power to save them is in your hand. Why me Lord? I asked? I said Lord this people can shout your name and they will be saved. Lord replied to me and said my child how can they remember my name in this situation. You have the authority given to you to confront the devil and his demon. The power had been given to you from above and you have been set apart to do the work. No one can save these people except you. The power to save them is in your hand. Go and save my people from the torment of hell. Go my daughter and prepare yourself to fight this battle for me. After Lord Jesus had spoken, He left, and I took my bible and left for the mission the Lord had sent me. I found myself in that building and I could hear people crying and screaming asking, "Who can save us from this torment?", the burden was too much to bear. Then I came into the house, and I began to challenge all the power of darkness with the fire of Holy Spirit. I said,

> "At the mentioned of the name of Jesus every knee shall bow, of those in heaven, those on earth and those under the earth and that every tongue shall confess that Jesus Christ is the Lord to the Glory of God the Father

(Philippians 2:9-11).

You that power of darkness that was tormenting these children of God, I command the Holy Ghost fire to consume you now." Fire came and burned the whole building, and every chain was broken, and that was how the people were saved.

9

MY EXPERIENCE AT WORK

I REMEMBERED THE INCIDENT THAT HAPPENED to my family in year 2001. The incident happened in the summer when I was about to graduate from college. I was getting ready to go to school one afternoon when Marshal from the court came knocking on our door. I did not want to open the door that day when one of the guys said, "We are Marshals from the court, and you had to leave this house right now". My father's wife who was in her bedroom that day did not allow me to open the door until the person was continuously knocking, then I opened the door. Then the marshal told us that we could not take anything from the house. So, I took my school bag and went to school. My father's wife took her luggage and went to her brother in Maryland. She did not even care about her family she left behind. That evening, I came back from school. My father and my younger brother stood outside the apartment door waiting to enter the house until they saw the notice marshal put on the door. Our neighbors were the ones who gave us accommodation in their apartment until we got ourselves together. After that morning, I did not see my father again. I was alone in the City of New York with no one to help. I did not know where my father and brother were at that time. I went back to church to see my pastor and Mrs. Adetola but I learned later that they had relocated to Maryland because they had a new parish. Two days later, when I came back to the apartment, the super called me and told me that two elders from Mountain of Fire Church came to look for me and the super told them what happened. They left their number with the super and told me to call them. I got the number from the supper, and I called them. Elder and Mrs. Faloye came and picked me and my luggage up to stay with them. The time I was with them, I told Elder and Mrs. Faloye that I wanted to work, and I did not want to be a burden for them, and I wanted to contribute to the bill in the house. Mummy and daddy Faloye always tell me no until I got myself together. I was there with them for three months, and when the time came, they sent to do a security training. I did the training for two weeks and I got a job. When I got my first salary, I paid tithe out of it and took the remaining balance to bank for saving until I had enough to stay on my own Four months later, I got a room for rent, and I went back to thank elder and Mrs. Faloye for all their loves support throughout my hardship. When I got to their house, I heard that they had traveled out of New York for crusade. Then in the year 2003, I met a young lady who usually picked up her three-year-old daughter from school and brought her to the place where I worked. I worked together at the same security company with this young woman and later along the line she told me that she was tired of staying in New York and wanted to go back to Nigeria. Then I asked her why? She then replied that she fed up because she had difficulties getting her legal documents to live in the United States. She stated that those men she met that wanted to help her with legal document stated that they had to sleep with her first before they could help her. She did not want to do that because she just wanted them to file for her and her daughter. So, she decided that she would return to Nigeria.

One day, during working hours, she called me and told me to guess what she was thinking about, but I said I cannot guess what you were thinking. She then told me that she wished she could get hit by a car or get involved in a car accident. Then I questioned why she had that thought in mind. She told me about her inability to get legal residency. She decided that she wanted to go back to Nigeria, but I told her do not to think about getting involve in car accident because I believe God would take control of her situation. Well, I did not know that the enemies already programmed what the woman had said, and her wish came to pass.

A STORM IN THE MIDST OF AN ACCIDENT

One winter, there was a snowstorm and that evening after closing for work I took my bag and went straight to the train station. Then the lady I worked with ran after me and called me to come back and the moment I came back to the office, she told me that her supervisor she worked with in the morning was coming to pick her up to drop her at home. She told me that she will ask her supervisor to drop me at home as well, but I told her that I would rather take the train. She said in this storming weather, and I replied yes but she said it was dangerous out there. So, both of us waited for her supervisor to come. Five minutes later, the supervisor came, and we locked the gate of the parking lot. The moment we got inside the car and left the parking lot to go on the street, I heard a boom sound. The car which packed on the left side of road drove out of the parking space and hit the van I was inside. The minivan tumbled three times and spun around till it reached the front of the Kings County Hospital. I got scared at the moment, and I thought within myself that the accident was the desire of the lady. I should have listening to the voice telling to leave and not wait but now it was too late for me. My mind was blank, and I could not think anymore. I knew that was how people die in a ghastly car accident the moment the van turned upside down. We could not get out of the car, and I could hear the lady scream her voice out. I knew this was her desire and it happened. The police and firefighter tried every possible way to open the door, but they could not. We still get stuck since the van still upside down. Tears rolls down from my eyes because the van still upside down and door could open but God was so good to me, and I did not know it until He sent His messenger to rescue me. I saw a bright light shone through the back of van I was, and I saw someone in a white bright garment stretched out his hand and the door opened. He took me by hand and brought me out of the van. The car turned and faced where it was going, and nobody knew how it happened. The angel turned the minivan to where it was going. The Lord had sent His angel to rescue but only things I saw on the floor was my body stay lifeless when the EMS took my body and my coworker to Kings County Emergency room. I knew that my spirit let my body the moment the angel came and rescued me from the midst of an accident. I kept following the angel until we reached The Great White Throne and the inscription was written on it. Ancient of Days was written on the Great White Throne. I saw 24 elders; they sat on throne and worshipped God day and night. I enjoyed everything the angel showed me. The way they worshipped God was different from the way we worshipped God on earth. I was enjoying the bit moment of life when the angel told me to let us go. As we were going, I could hear voices singing and shouting Halleluiah to the Lord but could not see those who were singing.

The more we got nearer, the more I heard the music. When I got there, I saw a lot of people in a white bright robe. They had crown of gold on their head with stars around it and nothing can compare with it. Their cloth linen was so bright and shining. I did not see a robe like that on earth, but I could hear them singing Halleluiah to the Kings of Kings and Lord of Lords. The angel told me that those saints I saw were waiting for the second coming of Jesus Christ and those who slept in the Lord will rise with Him. We continued our journey until I saw the New Jerusalem, the city and the foundation of the building was made of gold all around nothing can compare with it.

> "I saw a New Heaven and First Earth had passed away, there was no longer any sea. And I John saw the Holy City, The New Jerusalem, coming out of Heaven from God prepared as a bride dressed beautiful for her husband
>
> (Rev 21:1-2).

As we were going, I began to hear the people crying and asking God to get them out of there. The more we moved closer, the nearer I could hear their voices. Then we got to an open gate and Hell was written on it. Then I saw a woman begging to be saved, the fire burned her skin from head to toe. She had refused to accept Jesus Christ as her Lord and Savior even when the gospel was preached to her. The woman could see me but could not see the angel that stood beside me. She asked me for water to quench her thirst because the fire was too hot. There were other people in Hell as well; fornicators, adulterer, murderer, idolater, thief, unforgiving person, liar, witches, and wizard partake in Hell fire.

"There was certain rich man who was clothes in purple and fine linen and flared sumptuously every day. But there was a certain beggar named Lazarus, full of sores, who was laid at his gate, desiring to be fed with crumbs which fell from the rich man's table. Moreover, the dogs came and licked his sores. So, it was that the beggar died, and was carried by the angels to Abraham's bosom. The rich man also died and was buried. And being torment in Hades, he lifted up his eyes and saw Abraham afar off and Lazarus in his bosom. Then he cried and said, Father Abraham, have mercy on me and send Lazarus that he may dip the tip of his finger in water and cool my tongue; for I am tormented in the flame".

Luke 16:19-24.

It was so sad to see the rate at which many people were heading toward Hell fire. Pastors, deacons, deaconesses, church workers, elders, general overseers, bishop and many church members who worshipped God were among those who went to Hell Fire. The moment the angel stopped, I thought I had reached my destination, but the angel beckoned me to come along with him. There was a big signpost by the right with word written on it. Unless a Man Being Born Again, it cannot see the Kingdom of God. By the left sign of the post, it said that Wide is the road that led to destruction many people enter it. On the right small post, it said, "Narrow is the Gate that led to Heaven, and few Enter it". At the end of this left post there was a fearful demon there who was tall as an electric poll. He had an iron rod in his hand, his hair looked like that of a mad person and wore a kind of cloth that torn with short knickers. He was black and his teeth were like nails and his eyes were red like flame of fire. His own duty was to make Hah! Hah! Hah! continuously. There was an angel on the right, he wore a white garment. The garment was white, and nothing compared with it in this world. He had a very bolt belt made of gold and he wore a crown made of gold as well as stars around the crown. There in the front was a cross made of gold and the angel wore white gloves and golden shoes. His duty was to shout Halleluiah eternally. What really made me afraid was when I saw all those people who die coming and shivering and no one told them where to go. I saw uncountable people turning left and heading toward hell and no one told them to go there. I learned that nobody went in the right direction except few - only one person, or three sometimes. Among all the people who were going on the left, there were pastors among them, evangelist, elders, deacons, deaconesses, workers in the church, church members and unbelievers were all heading toward hell. When I got there, I saw the one on the left and I quickly ran to the right where the angel was shouting Halleluiah and I passed there.

10

WELCOME TO THE PALACE OF SALVATION

THERE WAS A WALL THERE AND I did not know where it came from. The wall was tall and made of gold. When you got to the wall, there was no handle to open it and no sign of door. The moment you get there, you just hear a boom, and the big wall opens by itself without anyone touched it. The moment I entered, the wall closed by itself and as I was going on my way, I saw a big house and something big was written at the entrance. YOU ARE WELCOME TO THE PALACE OF SALVATION. WE SHALL BESEECH YOUR SIN BEFORE YOU MOVE FORWARD. The moment I got to the entrance; the door opened by itself. As I entered, I saw those people who had died shivering. As I got there, I asked the people around to tell me what was going on and no one answered. The moment I got there, I saw an angel looking toward Heaven and never said a word. Suddenly you will just hear a voice from Heaven, and you would be called by your name. For example, Aderonke daughter of Jaiyeoba, you were saved in a particular year, particular month, particular week, day, hour, minutes, and seconds at this place. Before going forward, we shall beseech your sin and the moment your name is mentioned you will find yourself in front of the angel unexpectedly. The angel's face was big and round and the ray of light coming out of him looked like a flashlight. The angel would lower his eyes down and set his head and watch the person little by little until the person reached the toe of the angel. The ray of light coming out of the angel was like burning fire and it was like thrown the person in fire and the person will be crying Hah! Hah! Hah! When the person screamed, the angel would not pay the person any mind and he would just look at the person until he got to his toe. Immediately the person got to the angel's toe, there was a large screen by the side that looked like a television. The angel would look at the screen and every sin the person committed and failed to repent from before he died would appear on the screen. Sin like drinking, smoking, fornication, anger murderer and unforgiving spirit would appear on the screen. If the person failed to repent before he died, he would go to hell from there. The angel will look at the person and said Hah! Hah! Hah! pointed at the person's face and would say, "Why did you refuse to be cleansed by the Blood of the Lamb before you got here? The person would beg for forgiveness and the angel would shake his head and immediately a voice from Heaven would say depart and the storm will come from nowhere and carry the person to Hell.

There was an elderly man of God who came to the Palace of Salvation. This man served God for many years and what put him in trouble was anger. This man heard an argument with his wife and their neighbor already helped them to settle the quarrel. Whenever the woman offended this elderly man, he always remembered what his wife did to him in the past. Instead of forgiving and forget what his wife had done, he always got angry with her. When the man died and got to the Palace of Salvation, the angel did not allow him to enter. Immediately the anger appeared on the screen, the angel shouted pointed to the man of God and said "you servant of the most high God, you served God for so many years, why did you not allow the Blood of the Lamb to cleanse you from anger before coming here. The man said that it was the work of the devil. Then the angel said can you repeat the same thing when you see the devil? And the man of God said yes. Immediately, the devil came. He was tall and dark; his mouth was full of blood and had a cloth on. One part was red, and another part was black, and the devil said hah, hah, hah! why did you call me? The Angel said why did you not allow this man to get out of anger when he wanted to do it? Then devil said Hah! Hah! Hah! and turned to this man and said I wanted to ask you a question; you said you wanted to get out of anger, and I did not allow you. Look at this cloth, which one did I wear the day I did not let you get out of anger. The man did not know because one part was black, and the other was red and the devil left. Then I heard a voice from Heaven and the storm (Iji in Yoruba) came out of nowhere lifted the elderly man to Hell. The man screamed and said please had mercy of me, but the angel did not pay him any mind. The moment I saw that, I became afraid and fearful. After that I saw another room, but I had to pass through the wall to go through that door. The moment I walked to the narrow way I came to the Hall. In that Hall, I saw a tall, huge angel in a white glistening robe. His robe was so bright and radiant nothing can compare it. I never saw a white bright robe like that on earth. The huge angel stood by the corner of the room. He did not smile neither did he frown his face. He stood there and watched people all over the nation coming inside the room. The moment the door opened, I saw a wall between those two doors and immediately the wall opened, you will see the room.

11

HALL OF RESTITUTION

THIS ROOM WAS THE HALL OF Restitution and those people who did not make restitution before they died would end up going to Hell Fire. I saw all the people that died shivering and shaking the moment they entered the room because no one knew what would become of him or her the moment he or she entered. Those people who did not make restitution before they died would end up going to Hell from there. The storm would appear suddenly and threw the person in Hell the moment he or she had departed. Having seen this, I too was shivering as well because I did not know what would become of me. Then Lord Jesus appeared to me and said I should not be afraid and that He was there with me. The moment Lord said that, my fear disappeared, and I knew that the presence of the Lord was there with me. You my child must write everything you see and hear concerning my people. Lord showed me a woman who served Him all her life. The woman did not backslide, and she took her service for the Lord seriously, but her husband was wicked. The husband never attended church with her, and he was stingy with money. Her husband was very rich and anytime the woman asked him for money for cooking or children's tuition for school, he always gave her very little money. Then one day, when the woman gathered her husband cloth to laundry, she found a huge amount of money in his pocket. The woman took the money and spent it on food, and she did not tell her husband. The woman died and when she got to the Hall of Restitution, she was not allowed to go inside. The Angel at pole told the woman why she was refused to enter. He asked the woman why she did not tell her husband that she took the money from his pocket. The woman replied that she did not spend the money on herself, but she spent it on her family. Then the angel replied to her that even though your husband was wicked and stingy with money, that did not give you an opportunity to spend the money. The angel spoke again and said that was stealing because the money did not belong to you. Then this woman heard a voice from Heaven, "Depart! And the storm and whirlwind came and threw the woman in Hell. Even though she served God all her life, she still ended up going to Hell fire. Is there something in your life that you need to restitute before you die? Therefore, make adjustment before it is too late. If you think that you have taken things that do not belong to you, please return it before it is too late.

HALL OF FORGIVENESS

Three minutes after that, we came to another room and there was a word written on it. Welcome to the Hall of Forgiveness. Also, it was written that "**IF YOU DID NOT FORGIVE MEN THEIR TRESPASSES, NEITHER WILL YOUR HEAVENLY FATHER FORGIVE YOUR TRESPASSES. (Matthew 6:15).** If you have the spirit of unforgiveness you cannot enter that Hall. There was a man among those who came to the **Hall of Forgiveness** but was refused to enter because he had proposed in his heart never to forgive his wife for what she had done. The angel that stood at the door looked at the man and asked why you did not forgive your wife for what she had done. The man replied that he did not know that his life will be cut short like that. Then the angel replied to him that since you did not forgive your wife, neither your Heavenly Father will forgive you. Moment after that, I heard a voice from Heaven which said, "Depart!" And the storm came, carried the man, and then to Hell Fire. The man screamed and cried for help, but the Angel did not pay attention to him. After the Hall of forgiveness, we went to the **Hall of Accountability.**

HALL OF ACCOUNTABILITY

In this **Hall of Accountability** there was an Angel that folds his hand and does not say a word or laugh. On the other side not far away from where the Angel, was the four poles of pillars with a screen far away from where the angel was. At the bottom of the screen was something that looked like a typewriter or keyboard. When a person's name was called, the person would find himself in front of the Angel. Then something would force the person to stand in a position and the person will begin to talk about everything he or she had done on earth before the person died. The moment the person started talking, the computer began to type everything the person did on the paper. For example, the person would say that I so, and so person got this person pregnant and made her commit an abortion while on earth. The person would say, I so, and so robbed the bank and murdered so many people. When I was a witch, I so and so struck my friend's daughter with blindness, because I did not want her to make it in life. I wanted my daughter to be better than my friend's. When my friend's daughter got admission to college, I became jealous and I decided to take a revenge by killed her daughter while on earth. The person would mention all he or she did and after he or she had finished talking, then the typewriter would stop. The Angel would look at the screen and the paper would come out of the typewriter into the air and post the paper to four pillars. Then the person would go to that four pillars and begin to confess that it was true that he did all of those while on earth and he die. If the person forgot to say all he did, he would go back to the Angel and say "Sir, I forgot to mention that I did this or that. Then the typewriter would begin to type again until the person finished. If the person repented before he died and was washed by the blood of the lamb, the blood would appear from nowhere and erase all the sins the person committed. If the person did not repent before he died, he would go to Hell from that **Hall of Accountability**.

HALL OF VAIN

Now after all this, I found myself in the **Hall of Vain**. In this hall, every vain word a person uttered would be revealed. All the word that would be coming out of his mouth would be foolish words; lust word would just be coming out of the screen. The angel who stood at the entrance would just be looking. He would not say word to anyone. Any vain word altered, jokes the person mentioned while preaching in the church would appear on the screen. The person would try and stop talking but would be unable to do so. He would continue to alter those words until the screen was filled up. Whosoever repented or was washed by the Blood of Lamb would be cleansed from the vain word. The Blood of Jesus would come out of nowhere and would wipe off all those vain words the person had said if the person had repented and never went back to the vain words. Some people still go back to this vain word after being washed by the Blood of Jesus and in this case, the blood would just wipe off the part of the vain word the person had repented of. If the person did not repent at all, he would go from the Hall of Vain to Hell when he heard the word depart.

HALL OF GIVEN

In this Hall of Given, there was a big word written in front of the building. The word said,

"WILL A MAN ROB GOD, YET YOU HAVE ROBBED ME! BUT YOU SAY IN WHAT HAVE WE ROBBED YOU? IN TITHES AND OFFERINGS. YOU ARE CURSER WITH A CURSE FOR YOU HAVE ROBBED ME, EVEN THIS WHOLE NATION. BRING ALL THE TITHES INTO THE STOREHOUSE, THAT THERE MAY BE FOOD IN MY HOUSE, AND TRY ME NOW IN THIS, SAYS THE LORD OF HOSTS, "IF I WILL NOT OPEN FOR YOU THE WINDOWS OF HEAVEN AND POUR OUT FOR YOU SUCH BLESSING. THAT THERE WILL NOT BE ROOM ENOUGH TO RECEIVE IT".

(MALACHI 3:8).

In this Hall of Given, Christians that did not pay their tithe would go to Hell from the room. When you entered that room and the Angel in the Hall saw that you did not pay your tithe you would hear a voice from Heaven that would say, "Depart"! I discovered that the same eyes they used to look at a thief on earth were the same eyes the Host of Heaven use to look at a Christian who did not pay tithe. The thief on earth steals from people but a Christian who did not pay his or her tithe steals from God. So, if you have not been paying your tithe to God you are robbing Him, and you could end up in eternal destruction. Hell was not meant for people like us, but many had chosen the part they wanted to go. Many were being tormented by the demon because of their sin of fornication, adulterer, disobedient, unforgiving heart, idolatry greedy, covetousness, liar and murderer cannot enter Heaven. At one part of Heaven, there was children's room. Children had been placed in the room because they were aborted by their mothers. If the mother of that child died and went to Heaven, that child would scream and said, "My friends, my mother has come". The moment the mother came, the child would hug his or her mother. If the mother had repented and have given her life to Christ, the children would go back to their room. But if the mother, did not accept Jesus into her life and she came to Heaven, then the children would ask why she aborted the child, they would tell her what that child would have become in life whether, lawyer, doctor, accountant, nursing or engineering. These children would laugh and say they would do the same things the mother did to him or her. Then the children would rip the mother in pieces and would throw her in Hell. If you are accidentally pregnant, please do not abort it because it is detestable to the Lord.

There were 15 Halls before going to the **GATE OF HEAVEN**. As you are coming out to the last gate a white robe will come upon you without you notice it. From all the Hall that you passed, you did not where any cloth because you were naked. But when you leave the last Hall and about to set to the **Gate of Heaven,** you will not know when the clothe came upon you. Big word was written at the gate it was written big **WELCOME TO THE CITY OF THE KING OF GLORY, NO UNCLEAN THINGS WOULD PASSBY. WE SHALL BESEECH YOUR SIN**. The Angel at the palace had eyes inward and outward. All His body was full of eyes. The angel transparent and the glory in the Hall cannot be compared with and many Christian went to Hell from there. Before you entered the Gate of Heaven, there was a place where you will go to get the blood of Jesus. There was a Big Cross at the place and the moment you get there, you would see this Angel. Then a drop of the blood would be drop in your mouth and the blood would be coming out of your ear and eyes and mouth. After you got this Blood, the Angel would be welcoming you to Heaven. When it was my turned, and I got to the cross, the angel dropped a blood into my mouth. The blood came out through the nose and ears and as I came to the Gate of Heaven, the Angel accompanied me said, welcome to Heaven daughter of Most High God. The moment I entered, I shouted, Daddy, Daddy, Daddy Jesus I made it at last I am home. Then I saw Lord Jesus in His glorious appearance, He was so tall, and lied down among the twenty-four elders worshipped Him day and night. When Lord saw me, he said my daughter you made it welcome to Heaven. Lord carried me and said I am so happy you made it. Then again, I had the voice of the Lord and he said, my daughter writes everything you see and hear go and warn those people that are still alive to repent and come back to me. Let them know that Heaven is real so as Hell. All these people you see headed to Hell had chosen their own way. They did not repent before they die. Let those who are still alive know that there is hope for repentance to amend their ways. Then I replied again Father I am coming home at last. Then Lord Jesus said my daughter it is not time to come home. You must go back and tell my people what you see and hear concerning my plan for them. Many had chosen the part of destruction, but I am a merciful God. Did you know that the enemies wanted you to die at young age? But it is not my will for you to die young. There are still lot of things we need to do together. I am training you to be a useful vessel in my hand. You must go back because there are still work for you do to on earth. I had overcome the dead and I would be your God till your hair grows with age. I had speared the life of this young woman for your sake because you were in the same van with her. If you were not in the van, the young lady could have died and end up in Hell. "You are one of my children that is why I sent my Angel to stop the van from crashing". "Go my daughter and proclaim what the Lord had done for you. Go I am your God and I would be with you". I stood at the Throne of God and I saw a hand touched me but did not see anyone. I said, Father I wanted to see your face and God said no man see my face and live, but you can hold my hand. I remember in the bible when Moses said that he wanted to see God and God told him that he can only see His back. The voice of Lord said, my child I am with you always be ready for the manifestation of my work and I would always direct your steps. The Angel who came with me accompanied me back and we went out of the gate toward an opened field and then found myself in the midst of an accident with no broken bone. I was alive and well because God saved my life from that car accident. When I got to the hospital, the doctor at the emergency room discovered that we did not have any broken bones in our body. That was a miracle of how my Heavenly Father saved my life from that car accident and I am still alive today.

12

JESUS IS THE WATER OF LIFE

ONE NIGHT AFTER FINISHED MY PRAYER and bible reading, I went to bed. That night, I saw a bright white light that came through my window. I saw a vision, and in the vision, I came out of the house, locked the door when I saw an elderly woman approached me. The elderly woman asked me to give her water to drink but I did not have any water in the house. I told the elderly woman that I am going to the city to get water. The moment I finished spoken, Lord Jesus appeared to me in His glorious appearance and told me to give the woman the water. I replied and said, I am sorry Lord, but I did not have water. Then I saw Heaven opened and Angel of God coming out of Heaven in their white glistening robe and nothing can compare with the robe. The angel told me to follow him and as I was leaving, I was lifted up in spirit to a beautiful place. When I got to the place, I did not see the Angel anymore, but Lord Jesus stood beside me. Lord grasped me by hand, and we came to place where I saw a lot of people lining up but could not understand why the people were staying there. Lord Jesus looked at me and said my child come and see and the moment I got there, I saw a big rock at the corner and people used bowl to get water from the rock. Lord said, my child touched the rock and the moment I touched it and the water came out of the rock. I saw the excited people's eyes and the all gave their lives to Christ.

> And the Lord spake unto Moses saying, take the staff, and you and your brother Aaron gather the assembly together. Spake to the rock before their eyes and it will pour out its water. You will bring water out of the rock for the community so they and their livestock can drink. So, Moses took the staff from the Lord's presence just as he commanded him. He and Aaron gathered the assembly together in front of the rock and Moses said to them, listen you rebels must we bring water out of the rock?' then Moses raised his arm and struck the rock twice with his staff. Water gushed out and community and their livestock drank
>
> (Num. 20:6-10).

Are you thirsty or longing to change from your situation, please turned to Jesus before it is too late? He is the only one that can give you water of life freely. Salvation is free you do not have to pay for it because Jesus already done it. Jesus came to the world to die in your in your place. He paid the penalty for your sin. So, do not let it be too late. Jesus is the only way to Heaven. John 3:16 says that "For God so loved the world that He gave His Only Begotten Son that whosoever believe in Him should not perish but have everlasting life. God loved you so much that He does not want any of his children to perish. Have you ever thought of where you are going to spend your eternity? Heaven or Hell. Choose one because God does not want any of His children to go to Hell. Hell is prepared for the devil and his demon. Hell is not prepared for people like us. For those of you who did not believe in Hell you better believe before it is too late. You better believe that Hell is real it is a burning place till eternity. Heaven also is real it is like a paradise. Heaven is the Throne of God and a mansion place to live. In other to spend eternity with God, you must live a godly life, go for evangelism and soul winning and also spending your money for God will help you earn your crown to Heaven. If you are living in sin you must come to God in repentance and asked Him to forgive you and accept Jesus into your heart as your personal Lord and Savior. Choose Heaven! Before it is too late. Jesus loves you.

13

TWO ANGELS WITH TWO SPECIAL BOXES AND A GIFT BAG

AFTER ALL MY ENCOUNTERED WITH LORD Jesus in Heaven, I accompanied my Guardian Angel back and we were descending back to my room. That night, I found myself on the bed that night and I gave God all the glory and adoration for what He had done in my life. The following morning, I got up and prepared to go to school. When I got to school, I went to United Christian Fellowship Club and I conducted a bible studies with group of students. At the end of the session, most of the students asked for prayer request and I prayed with them. At the end of the day, some of students came back to me that their prayer was answered. During my prayer session, I met a woman who said, that she had been attacked by the demons and could not sleep in the night. We prayed together that Lord will intervene in her situation. When I got home that night, I took my Pray Rain Book I got from Dr. Olukoya and I began to pray on behalf of this woman. My prayer point was that "I bind every strongman in the life of this woman in the name of Jesus" I soaked her in the blood of Jesus and surrounded her with the Fire of the Holy Spirit. During the club hours we intercede together on her behalf and the end of it, she did not see those demons anymore. The Lord had delivered her from the hand of the devil. Two weeks later, I sat down outside school building enjoying the fresh air. I had a New Testament pocket bible in my hand. I was reading the book of psalms when I saw a bright light that shone toward my direction. The light was so bright, and I could not behold it anymore. I thought that the students who sat next to me saw the light, but they did not. My classmate looked at me and said Ronke, the sun was so bright. I told her that it was not the sun, but it looked as if someone turned the light on. As we were talking, I saw two men in a white bright garment, and they were descending from the ladder. I was wondering in my heart on how it was possible for me to see these two men in a white bright garment and my friends could not see them? The two Angels came toward me while I was talking to my friend and they motion me to be quiet and not say a word. Then I asked, is it possible for my friend to hear and see them? And one of them said no. But they can only hear me talking to myself. I asked them what they wanted from me and one of them said, I ran errand for Jesus and the other Angel said you know me very well. I am always with you and I said you are my Guardian Angel and He replied yes you right. What were those two boxes and a gift bag in your hand for I asked? The Angels smiled and said these two boxes and a gift bag were a gift from your Heavenly Father to you. The Angels dropped the two boxes and a gift bag in front of me. Inside the bag, I saw a letter written with Finger of God and I told the Angel I did not understand what was written on this letter. I asked the Angel to read what was written on the letter to me and one of them replies that this is between you and your Heavenly Father. We have no right to read the letter to you and the moment he said that, fear overshadowed me. Ten minutes later, my Guardian Angel said we had to go back now, and you must come with us. Why I asked? "The angel said it is an order from your Heavenly Father." Again, fear overshadowed me the moment we were heading toward Heaven because I was worried about what was written in that letter. Then I remember a passage in the Book of Daniel when King Belshazzar was feasting in his palace with his lords, wives and concubines using the gold vessels brought from Jerusalem in the temple. When they were feasting in the palace, there was writing on the wall and the king was troubled when he saw this writing. No one was able to understand the writing on the wall except Daniel. (Daniel 5:1-5). The Angels saw the fear in me and one of them said do not be afraid, I knew that something good would come out of it. Then He extend his hand toward me and said come along with me. I thought I was dreaming the moment that I extended my hand toward him, but I was not. As we got to Heaven, I saw a tall gold wall and it did not have a handle to open it. The moment we got to the wall I heard a boom sound and the wall opened by itself. I found myself in a big beautiful Hall and the building cannot be compared with anything. It was a beautiful Mansion that John described in the book of Revelation. I was going on the narrow way toward that beautiful Hall when Lord Jesus appeared in His glorious appearance my eyes could not behold him. He wore this beautiful white robe, and nothing can be compared with it. I never saw a white bright garment like that on earth. Lord said my child come with me and I followed him. I was taken to a poll and at the corner of that poll was a cross made of gold. Those who were being redeemed by the blood of the Lamb would go to that cross and were given the drop of the blood before entered Heaven. The moment I got to the cross, the Angel who stood by the cross put the drop of the blood in my mouth and the blood came out of my eyes and ear. I had been redeemed by the Lord. I still have the letter of God in my hand and I was so desperate to know what was written in the letter. I did not realize that the presence of the Lord was there with me even though I did not see Him; I could hear His voice and He said my daughter do not be afraid of what was written in that letter. There were 12 Pearl Gates and we went through of one them. At certain point, I saw myself at the throne of God. It was so amazing, when I saw different instrument at the throne of God. When the saints praised and worshipped God on earth and the praises reached Heaven, the throne of God, God's hear us. Our praise magnifies God, humbles us, motivates us, increases our joy, establishes our faith and elevates our emotion. Praises puts our focus on God, not on our problems. God's power, presence and ability transform our thinking. When we worship God, we gain a right view of ourselves. Praise deflates excess pride and ego. We gain a healthy self-image, based on God's view of us. By removing pride, praise strengthens us against temptation. If I love Christ, I will praise Him. If He has first place in my life, I will honor Him with worship and thanksgiving. Praise opens our hearts to want to live the way God desires holy and separated unto Him, to do His will above our own, to want to be like Him more than like anyone else. The more we worship Him, the more like Him we will become. Joy is the constant companion of praise. If we feel depressed or discouraged, praising God will soon bring us joy. The greater we see our God, the smaller we see our problem. Worry, fear, and doubt cannot survive for long in an atmosphere of praise. When our praised reached God's Throne, the whole Heavens rejoiced and When God heard the praised of His children, He then sent His Angel to deliver the message to any of His children. When our praises go up miracles come down. I was enjoying the view of God's Throne. The angel adored the One who sat on the Throne. They worshipped Him day and night. Even the twenty-four elders bowed to the throne of God. At certain point, I heard the Angels praised God with the sound of trumpet. The music they were playing were so amused to hear and worship the Kings of Kings and Lord of Lords. They were singing Halleluiah to the One who sat on the throne that was why the book of Psalms said:

Praise the Lord!
Praise God in His sanctuary;
Praise Him in His mighty firmament!
Praise Him for His Mighty acts;
Praise Him according to His excellent greatness!
Praise Him with the lute and harp!
Praise Him with the timbrel and dance;
Praise Him with stringed instruments and flutes!
Praise Him with loud cymbals;
Praise Him with clashing cymbals!
Let everything that has breath praise the Lord.
Praise the Lord!

(Psalms 150:1-6).

I still have the letter of God in my hand and I began to behold the beauty of the Lord. Each Angels in Heaven had their own assignment. They were always busy with the things of God. They ministered to the children of God and ran errand for God based on information he gave them concerning His children. Not long after that, Lord Jesus took the letter in my hand and said.

JESUS' LETTER TO ME

THE LOVING HAND OF YOUR FATHER IS OUTSTRETCHED TO YOU MY CHILD. DETERMINE TO DO ALL THAT I HAVE TOLD TO DO. SEEK, ASK, AND KNOCK AT THE DOOR OF MY SPIRIT. YOUR DETERMINATION WILL GENERATE STRENGTH. WITH REFLECTION YOU CAN SEE THAT MY LEADING HAS BEEN VERY GENTLE AND GRADUAL. YOUR PERSISTENT SEEKING WILL CREATE MORE DEFINITE REVELATIONS IN YOUR UNDERSTANDING. PURSUE AND YOU SHALL POSSESS. MY DEAR ADERONKE ONLY YOUR FAITH CAN LIMIT THE WORKS OF MY HAND. LOOK NOT AT CIRCUMSTANCES BUT LOOK UNTO ME FOR I WILL MAKE A WAY FOR YOU. NONE HAS EVER SOUGHT ME IN VAIN. I WAIT WITH A HUNGRY LONGING FOR YOU TO CALL UPON ME, I HAVE ALREADY SEEN YOUR HEART'S NEED AND I AM ALREADY PREPARING THE ANSWER. MY ANTICIPATORY LOVE IS A THING THAT MORTALS SELDOM REALIZE. DWELL ON THIS THOUGHT AND IT WILL EXPLAIN MUCH TO YOU. DISMISS FROM YOUR MIND THE THOUGHT THAT I MUST BE PETITIONED WITH SIGHS AND TEARS... YOUR THOUGHT OF ME NEED REVOLUTIONIZING. TRY TO SEE THAT MY LOVE FOR YOU IS SO GREAT THAT AS PLANS UNFOLD WHICH I HAVE MADE IT MEANS MUCH TO ME TO BE UNDERSTOOD. UNDERSTANDING MY LOVE FOR YOU WILL BRING GREAT JOY TO YOU FOR I AM THE LORD WHO LOVES AS NO OTHER.

EACH TICK OF THE CLOCK OF TIME BRINGS YOU CLOSER TO THE FULFILMENT I HAVE DESTINED FOR YOU. I SHALL NEVER FORSAKE YOU, MY DEAR CHILD ADERONKE. LO, I AM WITH YOU ALWAYS. GENTLY, LET ME REMIND YOU THAT I CARE ABOUT YOU, AND ABOUT YOUR NEEDS. YOU ARE MY GLORIOUS CREATION AND HANDIWORK. YIELD YOURSELF TO MY SPIRIT AND I WILL RELEASE THE FORCES TO CLEAR AWAY ROADBLOCKS. FOR IT IS MY DESIRE AND PURPOSE TO RESTORE LOVE AND BREAK DOWN BARRIERS BEFORE YOU, I AM THE LORD. REALIZE YOUR HIGH PRIVILEDGE IN THAT YOUADERONKE ARE MY LOVED CHILD. In those two boxes were special gift given to you and you must use them wisely. Those boxes contain, gift of healing, word of wisdom and working miracles. The same power that casts out devils is yours you must learn to use it and use it ceaselessly. The power to speak blessing into your life is in you, you must discover the ways to use this power as you daily seek me in prayer. After the Lord had spoken His word, I found myself in another part of Heaven. I saw the twelve Pearl Gate; I went through one of them with Lord Jesus. I sat down with the Lord and I enjoyed the beauty of Heaven. Then Lord began to teach me His word. After spending so much time with Lord, I found myself in my bedroom and I gave Him all the glory and honor for chosen me to become a vessel in His hand.

14

KEY TO OPEN HEAVENLY DOOR

I JUST FINISHED MY PRAISED AND worshipped one midnight and I fall asleep. Then around 3AM, I saw myself in the presence of the Lord. I was singing steadfast love of the Lord never ceasing and His mercy never come to an end. As I was singing, I saw the ministering Angel and they were ministered along with me. Later, I was accompanied by one of the Angel to Heaven. When a Small Gate opened, we entered. I went among those saints in a white bright garment. Their garment was so white I never saw a garment like that on earth. I could hear them shouting Halleluiah to the King of kings and Lord of Lords. I was so engrossed with the way these saints praised God and I saw that they were looking directly toward the sun light that shone in Heaven. The light was so bright that even I myself could not look toward that sunlight because it can blind my eyes. When I saw these saints, I saw that they were actually looked toward that light. I stood there looking at the saints shouting Halleluiah. The Angel who accompanied me told me that we must go and the Lord will tell me what to do. As we continued to walk, I met other saints and they were covered with the white garments. I asked the angel who was accompanying me, who were those people? The Angel replied that those were saints who slept in the Lord. Lord Jesus told them to leave them until His return. At certain point, I noticed the angel stopped and I did not see him anymore. I was left alone in the mist of Heaven. Five minutes later, Lord appeared to me in His glorious appearance and my eyes could not behold Him. He had bunch of keys in His hand and Lord Jesus beckoned me to follow Him and I did. When we got to a certain point, He stopped, and we went to a narrow way. When we got there, I saw a tall wall made of gold and the wall did not have a handle to open it. The wall opened by itself before we got there. As we crossed to the other side, I got to a room that was locked and only Lord Jesus had access to open that door. When I got to the front door, Lord gave me the keys and told me to open the door. The moment the door opened I could see the inside; it was so marvelous. I did not see the room like that one earth. The room looked like mansion and I asked Lord who room was this and Lord replied my child Aderonke, this room belong to you. The angels had been preparing building material for your home in Heaven. You earned this Heavenly material because of your soul-winning, for me. You were faithful with tithing according to the book of Malachi. You propagate the gospel by distributed the tracts and New Testament pocket bible to the church who did the prison ministry and many lives had been saved. You did great job of evangelism and by training your children to win soul for me. I am so proud of you my child and I want you to keep that good work. Never relent in doing good work and continued to do good and you would see the reward. I saw that many pastors, bishops and elders had a big mansion in Heaven for all their good work. When I saw the beautiful home, the Angel built for me, my name was written in front of the building. In that room, I saw so many rooms and the Lord told me that the rooms belong to my spiritual children. Those that I preached to and gave their life to him would inherit the room. Lord spoke again, my daughter, stay away from sin and live a holy life and you will enjoy the presence of your Heavenly Father. I knew that I did not deserved to be in the presence of the Lord, but He was so merciful and gracious to me. If I can experience the presence of the Lord who called me His child, you too an experience His presence when you accepted Him as your Lord and Savior. Please accept Jesus before it is too late so that you too can enjoy His presence.

15

MY LAST DAY IN HEAVEN

AFTER THE LORD HAS SPOKEN HIS word, I found myself in a beautiful garden and in the garden were beautiful flowers of different color. The moment, I touched the flower to smell, the flower shouted Halleluiah. I heard the voice of an Angel who told me that those flowers you see singing Halleluiah were waiting for the coming of the saints to come to Heaven. I went with the Lord to one of the Pearl Gates and we sat down and Lord Jesus began to teach me. I had a pen and a pad and I began to write everything the Lord had spoken to me in that vision. Three minutes later, I lifted in my spirit and found myself in my room. I thanked God for given me an opportunity to be in His presence and for chosen to be a vessel in His vineyard. I thought that I had completed all the mission the Lord had sent me to do but my journey never ends there. This is how it happened. One evening, I was in the kitchen cooking dinner when I heard someone called my name. I went to my father's room and I asked him if he called me and he said he did not call me. Then I heard my name again loud and clear Ronke and I did not answer. Fortunately, I went back to my room and I heard the voice again. Then I remembered that when I was young, I heard the same experience while I stayed with my grandmother and she told me a bible story about a boy named Samuel. (Samuel 3:1-10). When I sat down to do my schoolwork, I heard the voice again and Lord spoke, my daughter Aderonke you had not yet recognized my voice. Your mind was so preoccupied in whatever you were doing than listening and hearing my voice. When I realized that it was the Lord who called me, and I went on my knee and asked for His forgiveness for not paying attention to Him when He called me. That night, I did my prayer and went to -bed. Then around 3AM, Lord Jesus came in His glorious appearance but could not see His face. My eyes could not behold Him anymore because there was a bright light shone around me. The light almost made me blind when I looked toward it. Then Lord said, my child takes your bible, your notebook and pen then follow me. I took my bible and I followed him. Lord Jesus took my hand and we headed toward cloud and we went up. When we reached a certain place, we stop and sat down together. Where are we Lord, I asked? The lord replied my child you were in paradise. This would be a place where I and you we meet so that I can prepare you for the work I have for you ahead. Lord spoke again, I had chosen you from the womb to be a vessel in my hand. Now my child Aderonke takes your pen and paper and begins to write everything I would tell you. My child, tell my people that I Jesus Christ came to the world to die for their sin and on the third day I rose again. Many of my children have become a victim of Hell fire because of their disobedient. I did not create Hell fire for my children, but I created it for the devil and his demon. Let my people know that Hell is real and it is not my desire that any of them should perish. All my children need to live a holy life and stay away from sins like anger, fornication, adultery, backbiting, malice, murderer, thief, idolatry, unforgiveness and drunkard. Anyone found committed these sins would need to come to me in repentance because I am a merciful God. I would have mercy on who I would have mercy. I AM that I AM the Alpha and Omega, the Beginning and the End, the Omnipresence, Omnipotent, the Provider, Protector, the Shelter in the Storm, The Banner is Love, The Ancient of Days and that is my name. Many of the churches today are not preaching about Hell fire anymore. They did not warn their members and workers in the church about Hell and they are so busy preaching about financial freedom holiness without and within. Some of these people also consulted other power from outside beside the power of God.

After the Lord had spoken His word, I found myself another part of Heaven. I discussed before about seeing the Twelve Pearls Gate and we went through one of the gates. I felt the presence of God in my room. I saw Heaven opened and I saw the angels worshipped God day and night. They said you are the Lamb of God that can open the scroll that no one can open. God showed me who He is and touched me by His hand. God did not let me see His face and I told Him that I wanted to see His glory. God said, my daughter, no man sees my face and live. Then I remember in the Book of Exodus when Moses told God that he wanted to see His face.

And He said, I beseech thee, shew me "thy glory. And he said, I make all my "goodness pass before thee, and I will proclaim the name of the Lord before thee; and will be gracious, and will shew mercy. And He said Thou canst not see my face; for there shall no man see me, and live. And the Lord said behold, there is a place by me, and thou shall stand upon a rock: And it shall come to pass, while my glory passeth by, that I will put thee in a cliff of the rock, and will cover thee with my hand while I pass by: And I

will take away mine hand and thou shalt see my back part: but my face shall not be seen.

(Exo. 33:18-23).

God touched my hand and told me to go and proclaim the good news to His people. I was taken on a tour to Heaven. I saw a New Jerusalem coming down like bridegroom coming out of chamber. All nations shouted Halleluiah and praise the Almighty God and its Lamb in its Temple. On many occasions, I saw each angel in Heaven, had a huge job to do. Some of them came with a scroll in their hand pouring out judgment in the life of people who rejected the gospel of Christ. Those that committed murder, stealing, adultery, and cheating but never repented were judged according to their deeds. I was surprised to see how many people were being deceived by the devil. Many nations would be judged according to their work and the church of God also who be judged. Sheep and goat would be separated. God worked in mysterious way that He created individuals for His own purposes, and no one can comprehend Him. He did His own things for His own good. He was a merciful Father and forgave us when we come back to Him in repentance. Even when I knew that I am not worthy to be in His presence, He still set me apart for His work. God revealed Himself to me and showed me who He is. My experience with God began when I was 7 years old and He ministered to me through vision and dreams. I went on a tour with the Lord and experienced what I called divine revelation. Through Him I began to work signed and wondered where I found myself preached the word of God. I had been on a tour with the Lord on many occasions. At the age of 24, I had another experience with God and used me for His own purpose. If I can have encountered with Jesus Christ, you too can do the same. In order to have an encountered with Jesus Christ, you have to give your life to Him. That is how you will be able to enjoy being with Him. If you have read this book and you decided to give your life to Christ please pray this prayer and confess the following:

HEAVENLY FATHER,

I COME IN THE NAME OF JESUS CHRIST. I BELIEVE IN MY HEART THAT JESUS CHRIST IS THE SON OF GOD. I BELIEVE IN MY HEART THAT HE DIED FOR MY SINS; I BELIEVE THAT YOU RAISE HIM FROM THE DEAD FOR MY JUSTIFICATION. I RECEIVE HIM TODAY AS MY PERSONAL LORD AND SAVIOUR AND I GIVE GOD THE GLORY.

AMEN

When you pray this prayer God will begin to minister to you. If you want the presence of the Lord to be with you, you need to believe Him. Have faith in God and accept Him as your personal Lord and Savior. Tomorrow mighty be too late! Accept Jesus now. BEHOLD I STAND AT THE DOOR AND KNOCK, IF ANYONE HEARS MY VOICE AND OPENS THE DOOR, I WILL COME IN TO HIM AND DINE WITH HIM, AND HE WITH ME. IF YOU HAVE READ THIS BOOK AND YOU ARE SURE AND WILLING TO GIVE YOUR LIFE TO CHRIST, OPEN THE DOOR OF YOUR HEART TO HIM. JESUS IS KNOCKING THE DOOR OF YOUR HEART; INVITE HIM TO TAKE CONTROL OF YOUR LIFE BEFORE IT IS TOO LATE. DEVIL HAS NO GIFT TO OFFER YOU. DEVIL GIVES SICKNESS,

POVERTY, BARRENENSS, FAILURE AND DEMOTION AND WHEN GIVES ONE THINGS, HE REPLACE IT WITH ANOTHER. COME TO JESUS THE AUTHOR AND FINISHER OF OUR FAITH AND YOU WILL SEE A DIFFERENT. JESUS GIVES YOU SALVATION, MERCY, PROMOTION, FINACIAL BREAKTHROUGH, RICHES, HONOR, FAVOUR, JOY AND PEACE WHEN YOU PUT YOUR TRUST IN HIM. JESUS BECAME POOR SO THAT WE MIGHT BECOME RICH. HE PAID THE PENALTY FOR YOUR SIN THAT YOU AND I COMMITTED. WHY NOT TURN YOUR LIFE TODAY TO THE ONE WHO CREATED YOU AND CAN TURN YOUR SITUATION AROUND? HE WENT TO THE CROSS OF CALVARY AND TOOK AWAY YOUR SIN COME TO JESUS IF YOU NEED DELIVERANCE, COME TO JESUS IF YOU NEED HEALING, COME TO JESUS IF YOU NEED SIGNS AND WONDERS, COME TO JESUS IF YOU NEED PEACE, COME TO JESUS IF YOU NEED FINANCIAL BREAKTHROUGH, COME TO JESUS IF YOU NEED MIRACLE, COME TO JESUS IF YOU NEED FRUIT OF THE WOMB. COME TO JESUS IF YOU NEED A JOB, COME TO JESUS IF YOU NEED REPENTANCE LAST COME TO JESUS IF YOU NEED SALVATION AND COME TO JESUS IF YOU NEED LOVE. OUR GOD IS A LOVING GOD HE WOULD NEVER TURNED ANY OF HIS CHILDREN AWAY. EVEN IF THE WORLD FORSAKES YOU JESUS WOULD NEVER FORSAKE YOU. COME; COME, COME, TO JESUS BEFORE IT IS TOO LATE. HE IS KNOCKING AT THE DOOR OF YOUR HEART. OPEN THE DOOR OF YOUR HEART AND LET JESUS COMES IN. HE IS WAITING FOR YOU. THE BRIDEGROOM IS WAITING FOR YOU. DO NOT DELAY ACCEPT HIM! TOMORROW MIGHT BE TOO LATE. ACCEPT HIM today.

PART 11

SPENDING TIME ALONE WITH GOD

INTRODUCTION

IN 1KING 18:20-40 THE PROPHET ELIJAH is an amazing example of what can happen when believers pray with authority, when they come confidently to God asking Him to do something that glorifies Him. With the people of Israel and the prophets of Baal gathered at Mt Carmel for a "show-down" between the Lord and Baal, Elijah confidently prayed.

> **Lord God of Abraham, Isaac and Israel, let it be known this day that You are God in Israel and I am Your servant, and that I have done all these things at Your word. Hear me, O Lord, hear me, that this people may know that You are the Lord God, and that you have turned their hearts back to you again**
>
> **(1King 18:36, 37).**

When Elijah had finished his prayer, the fire of the Lord fell and consumed the sacrifice, as well as the wood, the stones, the dust, and all the water in the trench. When the people saw what had happened, they fell on their faces and said, "The Lord, He is God! The Lord, He is God!" Elijah did not pray in secret, off in some corner where nobody could see or hear him. He prayed openly and publicly. There was nothing tricky or shady about what he did; there was no doubt what he said. God tells us to come boldly into His presence. He grants us the privilege to come before Him with authority because of our position in Christ Jesus. We are to be bold in our faith that God will do what He desires to do and what He says He will do.

The New Testament tells us, "For we do not have a High Priest who cannot sympathize with our weaknesses, but was in all points tempted as we are, yet without sin. Let us therefore come boldly to the throne of grace that we may obtain mercy and find grace to help in time of need" (Heb. 4:15, 16), and, "let us draw near with a true heart in full assurance of faith" (Heb10:19). We have God's invitation; will we accept.

CONTENT

15

THE BENEFIT OF PRAYER AND FASTING

WHEN GOD CALLS US TO PRAYER and fasting, He always does so for our benefit. The Scriptures point out at least seven benefits to prayer and fasting.

1. Our attitudes, feelings, and thoughts get sifted pruned and purified so that God might entrust us with a greater ministry. By fasting and praying, we become more disciplined toward the things of the Father. We give Him opportunity to cut away from us those things that will slow us down or keep us from His plans and purposes.

2. We are able to discern more clearly the will of God for our lives. Fasting clears our spiritual eyes and ears so we can accurately discern what God desires to reveal to us.

3. We are confronted with our sins and shortcomings so we might confess them to God, receive forgiveness for them, and walk in greater righteousness. Many times, we break stubborn sinful habits when we fast and pray. Fasting and

prayer cleanse us and purify us from the errors that have kept us entangled with sin and folly.

4.   We experience a release of supernatural power. Genuine fasting and prayer result in spiritual growth, including a renewed outpouring of supernatural power. Certain problems and situations cannot be resolved except by fasting and prayer.

5.   We can influence national issues and concerns through our prayers. As we fast and pray for our nations, God will move. He will pour out His Spirit, in His ways and in His timing. We can count it.

6.   We can help build up God's people. Prayer is the generator of the church. It gives power to church ministers. It propels outreach to the lost. It creates a climate in which evangelistic efforts succeed.

7.   Our minds are sharpened. When we fast and pray, we begin to understand the Scriptures as never before. We become sensitive to God's timing and direction, with an increase awareness and ability to discern. We become keenly aware of what God desires to do and accomplish not only in our lives, but also in the lives of those around us.

16

THE MANY FACES OF PRAYER
COLOSSIAN 1:9-12

CHARLES FINNEY, A NINETEENTH CENTURY AMERICAN Evangelist, sometimes wrestled with what to say in prayer. One day a woman acquaintance felt deadly ill. She did not know Christ, but her husband asked Finney to pray for her. Finney immediately became burdened for the woman, but he did not know how to pray. Eventually, after grasping for right words, Finney received a breakthrough. He said he "was enabled to roll the burden upon" God and that he immediately felt sure that woman would not die. Not long afterwards, the woman made a full recovery and committed her life to Christ. There is much more to prayer, however, than a passionate plea for God to intervene. Paul often sprinkled his letters with intriguing prayers. We find one of them in Colossians 1: 9-12. In seven requests, Paul covers every area of our lives that needs the daily touch of God:

✸ *May we be filled with the knowledge of His will in all wisdom and spiritual understanding (v.9).* Ask God to fill you with the spiritual understanding you need as you walk in His will and study His Word.

* *May we walk in a manner worthy of the Lord Jesus Christ (v.10).* Jesus lived a blameless life, exactly what we should pursue.

* *May we please God in all respects (v.10).* Paul encourages believers to live a life pleasing to God and to excel in their Christian walk.

* **May we bear fruit in every good work (v.10)** We prove we are Jesus' disciples when we bear fruit

* **May we increasingly grow in the knowledge of God (v.10).** We should ask for more and more knowledge from His tremendous resources.

* **May we be strengthened with all might, according to His glorious Power (v.11).** Ask God to strengthen you to do His will for His glory and He will do it.

* **May our lives express joyous thanks to the Father for His grace to us (v.12).** Our love for Him should run so deep that we can't help but give glory and honor to Him.

So, what is prayer? Prayer is a means of communication with God (Ps 54:2) "Hear my prayer, O God; listen to the words of my mouth. When you felt like words could express what was in your heart, what is God's provision for you in such a time? Jesus makes prayer a high priority during his earthly ministry (Lk. 6:12). The parable of the tax collector and the Pharisee reveals that the prayers of the humble are heard by God and righteousness comes through humility. A Pharisee stands up probably in the center of the temple area where he can be clearly seen, and he proceeds to pray "about himself" (Luke 18:11). He is quick to compare himself to others, lifting himself up and listing all his good deeds. The tax collector, on the other hand, stands at a distance, away from the center of attention. He compares himself God's holiness, and, seeing his unworthiness, he cries out to God for mercy. Which man leaves the temple justified? The tax collector. "For everyone who exalts himself will be humbled and he who humbles himself will be exalted" (Lk. 18:14). Humility is the key to righteousness and to answered prayers.

When you pray, you approach God Himself. That knowledge alone should make you humble. The wonderful result of humility is that God's grace is released (Pr 3:34). God's grace, offered through Jesus Christ, gives you the confidence you need to approach God's holy throne (Heb 4:16). God desires to hear you and answer you. Go to Him in prayer right now. Throw off everything that hinders humility. Enjoy God's presence and believe that He hears and will answer you when you call out to Him. (2 Ch 7:14; Ps 6:9).

17

HOW TO PRAY WITH AUTHORITY
1 KING. 18:20-40

Prophet Elijah is an amazing example of what can happen when believers pray with authority, when they come confidently to God asking Him to do something that glorifies Him. With the people of Israel and the prophets of Baal gathered at Mt. Carmel for a "showdown" between the Lord and Baal, Elijah confidently prayed:

> **Lord God of Abraham, Isaac, and Israel, let it be known this day that you are God in Israel and I am Your servant, and that I have done all these things at your word. Hear me, O Lord, hear me, that this people may know that you have turned their hearts back to You again**
>
> **(1 King 18:36-37).**

When Elijah had finished his prayer, the fire of the Lord fell and consumed the sacrifice, as well as the wood, the stones, the dust, and all the water in the trench. When the people saw what happened, they fell on their faces and said, "The Lord, He is God! The Lord, He is God!" Elijah did not pray in secret, off in some corner where nobody could see or hear him. He prayed openly and publicly. There was nothing tricky or shady about what he did; there was no doubt about what he said. God tells us to come boldly into His presence. He grants us the privilege to come before Him with authority because of our position in Christ Jesus. We are to be bold in our faith so that God will do what He desires to do and what He says He will do.

The New Testament tells us, "For we do not have a High Priest who cannot sympathize with our weaknesses, but was in all points tempted as we are, yet without sin. Let us therefore come boldly to the throne of grace, that we may obtain mercy and find grace, to help in time of need" (Heb. 4:15-16), and, "let us draw near with a true heart in full assurance of faith" (Heb. 10:19). We have God's invitation; will we accept it?

18

WE STAND TALLEST AND STRONGEST ON OUR KNEES
DAN 6:10-11

AN OLDER PASTOR GOT INTO THE habit of challenging his congregation by quoting Jeremiah 33:3: "Call to Me, and I will answer you, and I will tell you great and mighty things, which you do not know." Leveling his eyes at those gathered before him, he would say, "Try it. It works!" This is a very simple thought, but it carries a tremendous truth. God wants us to call to Him. Many times, He allows disappointment to rake through our lives so that He might draw us closer to Himself. Prayer is the most powerful tool a believer has; nothing compares to it. In prayer we profess our need of Christ and His solution to our problems. In prayer we learn to worship Him and grow spiritually in His loving presence. Do not worry about what to say; the Holy Spirit will show you. Tears are just as effective as words at time, and God is sensitive to every tear you cry. Just as He understands the hurt you feel, so He knows how to deal with and guide you through any anger that has penetrated your life.

God is bigger than any problem you face. He knows the way before you, and only He can guide you through the difficulty. When trial hits, always respond first by going to Him in prayer. As you pray, hope invades your life and fills you with the reassurance of His undergirding presence. Several things are essential to establishing a powerful prayer life. One is to choose a definite time to spend in prayer. Setting a time, whether early in the morning or late in the evening, is not the issue. Consistency is the key here. Ask God to show you the perfect time when you can be alone with Him, even for fifteen minutes. God honors the prayers of His people! If you come to him, He will provide all you need for your prayer life. If possible, select a place where you can be alone with Him. You may need to consider obligations with younger children. When it comes to prayer, you will find that God is very creative; He will provide the perfect place for you to seek Him. Making the commitment to pray is an essential step. This alone tells God that your heart is open to His heart and that you want to learn more about Him and the life He has planned for you.

As we spend time with Him, God lovingly teaches us how to pray and how to listen for His still, small voice as He replies to our humble requests. Prayer is the doorway to blessing and freedom from bondage. As we pray, God teaches us more about Himself and the spiritual warfare needed to combat the enemy. Every day God calls us to put on the armor of God and to stand firm in our faith (Ephesians 6:10-17). The only way to do this is through prayer and complete reliance on Jesus Christ, who is Lord overall. An older pastor tells his congregation that the distance between success and failure, and victory and defeat, is about six to twelve inches, or whatever the distance, it is for you to drop to your knees and pray to your wondrous Lord and Savior. You never stand taller or stronger than while on your knee! Over your lifetime, you will face many difficult situations. Some will feel very exciting and challenging. Whatever life sends your way, you can be sure that God cares. He enjoys seeing you excited over His blessings, and He mourns with you when tragedy strikes. A man of God says, over the years, I have enjoyed keeping a journal that contains many prayers and God's insights for each request. You can do the same thing by writing out your need and the way God answers your prayers. Pray that He will provide specific verses that apply to your situation. Look for His promises in His Word. Claim them, write them down, and trust Him. You will never be disappointed!

My challenge to you is simple: Whatever you are facing, trust God with it. Ask Him to take away anxiety, fear and feeling of frustration. When you trust the Lord, you rest in His care. You probably could name at least one place where you feel safe and accepted. But there is no place where you will feel more accepted and secure than in the presence of God. All of this and much more wait for you as you come to Him.

19

WHAT IS OUR AUTHORITY IN PRAYER?
2 CHR. 20:3

ONE DAY, KING JEHOSHAPHAT AND THE people of Judah saw that a great multitude had risen up against them. Three groups of aggressors: the Moabites, the Ammonites and the people of Mount Seer, launched a major assault against Jerusalem. Jehoshaphat felt deeply afraid, but rather than cower in fear, he "set himself to seek the Lord" (2 Chr. 20:3). He proclaimed a fast throughout all Judah and called the people together to join him in seeking the Lord. He stood before the people in the house of the Lord and prayed, "O Lord God of our fathers, are You not God in Heaven, and do You not rule over all the kingdoms of the nations, and in Your hand is there not power and might, so that no one is able to withstand You?" (20:6). Jehoshaphat did not express doubt in the power of God, but rather publicly proclaimed his trust in the Almighty God. He declared that he was putting all of his hope in the Lord of unlimited power. In addition, Jehoshaphat stated very plainly that he, even as king of

Judah, was standing in total humility and weakness before the Lord. He claimed no authority in or for himself. He said to God:

* You are the One who gave us this land.
* You are the One who has allowed Your people to dwell in it and build a sanctuary in it.
* You are the One who said that we should cry out to You in our affliction and You would hear and save us.
* You are the One who told us to spare these enemy people when we first came to occupy this land.
* You are the only One who is capable of judging these enemies who are rising against us; we have no power and no plan.

He concluded his prayer by admitting, "our eyes are upon you." In effect, Jehoshaphat was saying, "If you do not exercise Your authority in this matter, we are doomed. We are putting our entire trust and confidence in You and You alone." We see no trace of egotism in Jehoshaphat. He made no demand that God do something that God did not desire to do. Jehoshaphat claimed no authority in himself and no power for himself. But he wisely recognized that all power and all authority rest in God alone, and from that understanding, he petitioned the God of Heaven.

ASK GOD FOR SPECIFIC THINGS

Many Bible passages challenge believers to ask God for very specific things. Read the following familiar verses to remind yourself how important it is to ask God for the things you need. God expects you to ask!

❊ At Gibeon the Lord appeared to Solomon in a dream by night; and God said, "Ask! What shall I give you?" (1 King 3:5).

❊ [Jesus said,] "Whatever things you ask in prayer, believing, you will receive." (Matt 21:22)

❊ [Jesus said,] "Until now you have asked nothing in My name. Ask, and you will receive, that your joy may be full." (Matt 16:24).

❊ If any of you lacks wisdom, let him ask of God, who gives to all liberally and without reproach, and it will be given to him. But let him ask in faith, with no doubting, for he who doubts is like a wave of the sea driven and tossed by the wind. (James 1:5, 6).

If we were to summarize these verses, we would find some very clear and concise principles related to our asking:

❊ God wants us to ask Him to meet all of our needs.

❊ God delights in revealing to us His desires and His ways of doing things.

❊ We can ask God for all things, including those that relate to the natural world.

❊ We are wise to ask in agreement with others.

❊ We must always ask in faith and in the name of Jesus.

❊ God will respond to our need not in a way that opposes His commandments, but in a way that pleases Him and brings Him glory.

✻   We can be assured that whenever we ask God for something, He hears and responds to us, giving us precisely what we think we need, but which always benefits us most.

The Bible tells us, "You do not have because you do not ask" (James 4:2). For what things in your life have you failed to ask God?

20

WHY DOESN'T GOD ANSWER MY PRAYER SOONER?
GEN 45:25 - 46:4

IF GOD HEARS OUR REQUESTS AND loves us so much that He sent His own Son Jesus Christ to die for us, then why does it appear to take Him so long to respond to some of our most urgent requests? Carefully consider the following ten reasons why there may be delay in our prayer:

Our disobedience - our sin can prompt God to withhold His gracious hand (Ps 81:10-12). When we disobey His commands and refuse to repent, He sometimes stops His ears from hearing our requests.

Our doubt - Without faith, no one who asks anything of God will receive what he requests (James 1:5-8). But with faith all things are possible (Mark 9:23).

Our attempts at manipulation- if we try to control or manipulate God, we should not expect answers to our prayers (1Sam. 13:9-14). He is the Master; we are the servants.

Wrong motivation- Neither self-centered requests nor those tingled with evil intent will receive an answer (James 4:3). God refuses to partner with our lusts or our schemes.

Our lack of responsibility- God cannot be expected to compensate for a lazy or negligent person (Prov. 19:15). The Lord has His work to do; we have ours.

An illegitimate "need"- is this thing you want really a need, or is it something that you have illegitimately come to expect? Often, we have bigger eyes than stomachs (Jer. 45:1-5).

Rejecting God's method- Do not turn away a means of supply merely because it does not fit your expectations or criteria (Josh. 6). A man named Naaman almost made this mistake and it would have cost him his health (2Kin. 5:8-14). God's redirection- Sometimes God is in the process of redirecting us or preparing us for something new (Gen 37, 39-50). God loves to do fresh, exciting things with His people (Is. 43:19). God's desire to teach us- God may want us to focus on our spiritual and eternal needs so that we will learn to trust Him in all things and for all things (Is. 48:18). God's desire to bring us to repentance- God may want us to own up to our sin, confess it, and repent of it (Luke 15:11-31). And even when God delays His answers, He instructs us to keep on praying (Luke 18:1-8) Prayer is life's greatest time saver, even when it does not seem like it.

PRAYER IS LIFE'S GREATEST TIME SAVER
2 THESS. 3:1

When Pastor Stanley and his family moved to Atlanta, Georgia, they could not seem to find the right house. It took them more than a month before they found a house, they felt good about. In the meantime, they had been living with friends. As you can imagine, they were ready for a place of their own. They prayed and applied for a loan. They asked God every day to get the loan approved. They really believed He would; they thanked Him in advance. One week later, the banker turned down their loan request. What a shock! He just could not imagine why. And they could not understand what God was up to. "Why God did not answer their prayer?" They asked. God answer their question the following day by sending a tremendous rainstorm. The basement of the house they almost bought was flooded with a foot of water. They planned to use it for a study and for storage. But God was watching out for them. One week later they found the right house, and they enjoyed living there for eight years.

Prayer not only spared them a lot of trouble, it saved them a lot of time. God's answer seemed like a delay to them, but in fact it kept them from wasting countless hours trying to fix a defective house. Prayer really is life's greatest time saver. Jesus spoke of this relationship between an apparent delay in God's answer to our prayers, and the fact of how it actually saves us time. In Luke 18 He told a parable to teach us "that" men always ought to pray and not lose heart" (v.1). That does not sound like a passage on how prayer saves time, does it? Yet at the end of His story, Jesus explained His point like this: "And shall God not avenge His own elect who cry out day and night to Him, though He bears long with them? I tell you that He will avenge them speedily" (Luke 18:7-8). Did you catch it? God may "bear long" with us in our prayers, and yet He is committed to acting on our behalf "speedily." That means that prayer really is life's greatest time saver, for God will answer our prayers as soon as it is best for us not one moment sooner, not one second later. What may feel like a delay to us is actually God sparing us tremendous amounts of wasted time. God waits for us to grow spiritually in some areas before He gives us all spiritual and material blessings He has in store (Ephesians 1:3). God will answer our prayers as soon it is best, not one moment sooner or one second later. This is why prayer really is life's time saver.

21

HOW CAN I MAKE MY PRAYER LIFE FRESH AND NEW JEREMIAH 33:1-3?

PROPHET JEREMIAH WAS NOT A POPULAR man. When he declared the truth, God had given that Judah would soon start seventy long years in captivity, his people imprisoned him. Yet in such a dire circumstance, Jeremiah learned something profound about prayer. Jeremiah 33:1-3 says: "The word of the Lord came to Jeremiah a second time, while he was still shut up in the court of the prison, saying, 'Thus says the Lord who made it, the Lord who formed it to establish it (the Lord is His name): "Call to Me and I will answer you, and show you great and mighty things, which you do not know." Prayer is a very real part of a vital relationship with God. It is not for some special spiritual elite; it is for you. Three principles within these verses can transform your old notions about prayer into something fresh and new. First, God says, "Call to Me." He wants to hear from you. His all-loving, omnipotent heart desires to hear your innermost thoughts and feelings. He wants to hear from you in the hard times and when life is going smoothly. In fact, your sweetest times of prayer happen when you come before Him simply to praise and worship and give thanks for what He has done. Second, God says, "I will answer you.

SEEKING GOD'S GUIDANCE

Psalm 27:14 "Wait on the Lord; be of good courage and He shall strengthen your heart; Wait, I say, on the Lord!" Life is full of choices and if we want to make the right choices, we need God's guidance to choose those that glory God, benefit us, and others. All of us will eventually come to places and times when we will desperately need God's guidance. How can believers find that guidance? Seven words may help.

1. Cleansing: we need to ask, "Is anything in my life hindering me from hearing what You are saying? If so, what is it?" Cleansing comes by confession (1 John 1:9) "If we confess our sins, He is faithful and just to forgive us our sins and cleanse us from all unrighteousness."
2. Surrendering: Submitting to the will of God is both humbling and an uplifting experience (1Peter 5:6) "Therefore, humble yourself under the mighty hand of God that He may exalt you in due time.
3. Asking-God promises that when we ask according to His will, He hears us. And when we know that He hears us, we know He has answered, even though the answer may come over a long period of time. (1John 5:14-15)

4. Meditating: God promises that His Word will be a light to our paths (Ps 119-105), so the more we think about His Word, the clearer our path will become

5. Believing: In Mark's Gospel, we learn that when we ask, we must believe He is going to give us what we have requested (Mark 11:22-24)

6. Waiting: God promises that He acts on our behalf when we wait on Him (Is.64:4). If we want to, we can run ahead of Him, dash in and try to fix things on our own or manipulate circumstances. On the contrary, if we wait on the Lord, then our sovereign, divine, omnipotent God will act on our behalf. It is our choice.

7. Receiving: When we obediently seek the will of God, we can be sure that He will hear us and give the wisdom we need to make the right life choices (Matt. 7:7-8; James 1:5).

You will find great peace and confidence in knowing that you are making choices based on God's guidance. Perhaps no one else will understand or agree with your decision but you will have heard from the One who matters the most.

22

PRINCIPLES FOR EFFECTIVE INTERCESSION

JAMES 5: 15-16 "AND THE PRAYER of faith will save the sick, and the Lord will raise him up. And if he has committed sins, he will be forgiven. Confess your trespasses to one another, and pray for one another, that you may be healed. The effective, fervent prayer of a righteous man avails much." We cannot obey a multitude of God's commands without being in regular, close fellowship with other believers. He has designed this world so that many of our needs are met only through mutual interdependence. Each of us has prayed for others without seeing results. When that happens, it is easy to get discouraged. Rather than give up, we should review our lives to see if we need to alter something. Our prayers must flow from a heart filled with love, compassion, and forgiveness. Our prayer we fail if our heart is full of bitterness, resentment, or anger. Pray first that you might have God's love and compassion for others, and then that you might forgive them fully. We must recognize that our prayers are the link between another's need and God's inexhaustible resources. You must ask the Lord to reveal to you the true needs of a person, not just the superficial or symptomatic needs. Ask Him also to reveal to you the greatness of His love and power and help you desire to meet those needs. We must identify with the need of the other person. Compassion feels the full depth of another's need. When we see people as truly hurting, bleeding and agonizing on the inside; when we see them with the eyes of Jesus, our compassion gets released and we pray with a new degree of understanding and depth of emotion.

We must desire the highest good in person's life. God may not reveal to us His highest good for another person, but we can make it our prayer, nonetheless. We do not need to know exactly what God wants to bring to pass. Ultimately, God's highest good is *wholeness*. Wholeness includes vibrancy and life in every domain: spirit, mind, body, emotions, relationships, and finances. We must be willing to be part of the answer in meeting the person's need. If you pray for another but remain unwilling for God to use you to meet that person's need, God will not hear your prayer. Jesus touched the lepers, the unclean, the desperate sick, the dead. He never backed off from people in need, nor did He pass them on to someone else. We are to follow His example. We must be willing to persevere. We must keep on praying, regardless of whether we see immediate results. The longer we pray for a person, the more tightly our hearts will be knit to him or her. Prayer binds us together with spiritual glue far stronger than anything man can create. Such a bond lasts into eternity.

HOW CAN I LEARN TO PRAY EFFECTIVELY?

Daniel demonstrates how to pray with both power and confidence. When he discovered in the book of Jeremiah that the Babylonian captivity would last seventy years (Daniel 9:2), he fell on his knees and began to intercede for his people (Daniel 9:4-19). In Daniel 9, we see a great example of what prayer should be. Its focus is on almighty God and His character. It includes sincere confession, unselfishness, and dependence on the Word of God. Such prayer has great power. In Daniel's case, God sent the angel Gabriel with His answer even before the prophet had completed his supplication. To find God during your own hardship, go to the portal Daniel knew best. Go to your knees. Model your prayer after Daniel's and model your life after Daniel11:32: "The people who know their God shall be strong and carry out great exploits."

The Bible tells us, "The effective, fervent prayer of a righteous man avails much" (James 5:16) We want our prayers to be exactly effective, especially in a crisis. When we meet God's requirement, we can feel confident that He will act in our situation as a result of our earnest prayers. What are those requirements of Fervent prayers? Fervent prayers are filled with passion and a strong sense of personal helplessness. They also have a narrow focus on some specific difficulty. Scripture calls this type of prayer "laboring fervently" (Col 4:12). Righteousness: At salvation, we become rightly related to God as His children. He permanently seals us with the Holy Spirit and declares us righteous forever because of our position in Jesus Christ. But the Bible also uses the word "righteous" to describe a believer's conduct. This means that to be called a "righteous person," we must be found in Christ (Phil 3:9) and it a habit to obey God (Eph.4:1; Col. 1:10). If we willingly and knowingly engage in sin, then we do not live righteously, and our prayers will lack power. When the Lord hears the impassioned prayer of a righteous person whose life reflects God's way, Scripture promises that the Holy Spirit will begin His divine work. God responds with great power to the prayers of even one righteous person. Friend, that person can be you!

EFFECTIVELY TACKLING A PRAYER BURDEN

When Nehemiah heard that his people lived in great and reproach, that the walls of Jerusalem lay in ruins, and the gates of the city remained burned and broken, he responded with prayer: "I sat down and wept, and mourned for many days and I said: 'I pray, Lord God of Heaven, O great and awesome God, You who keep Your covenant and mercy with those who love You and observe Your commandments, please let Your ear be attentive and Your eyes open, that You may hear the prayer of Your servant which I pray before You now, day and night." (Neh. 1:4-6). Nehemiah was experiencing a prayer burden. **A prayer burden** can be defined as a strong motivation to pray for others and to carry the needs of others before God in prayer until God responds. The Bible has a great deal to say about burdens. We are to bear one another's burdens (Gal 6:2). We are to go the second mile in helping another person (Matt 5:41). Much of our ability to bear natural burdens is derived from developing our ability to carry spiritual burdens in prayer.

A sense of spiritual weight usually accompanies a prayer burden- a heaviness of heart, a drag on one's emotion, a spirit of mourning, or a feeling of restlessness that we cannot seem to shift ourselves away from a problem or need that has come to our attention. God does not act in many situations because we do not pray. God waits for either the co- instigator of the negative situation to cry out to Him for forgiveness, or for the victim of the negative situation to cry out to Him for mercy. Then He will act. If you feel burden to pray for another person, God desires to act on that person's behalf. He places the burden to pray on your heart, and He moves through the opening. As you pray, you can get in on the blessing that God has for that person through an answered prayer.

23

FIGHT ALL YOUR BATTLES ON YOUR KNEES AND YOU WIN EVERY TIME

2 SAM. 15:31 "AHITHOPHEL IS AMONG the conspirators with Absalom." The term resistance movement describes situations in which oppressed people revolt against their oppressors. Resistance fighters take stance, "I am not going to stand idly by and allow this evil to continue. I choose to resist the wrongs. Whether I live or die in resisting my oppressor, I will no longer live as I have been." Such is the case of Ahithow2sw2a1qʻphel in 2 Samuel 11:3 compare with 2 Samuel 23: 24, we learn that Ahithophel was Bathsheba's grandfather. Apparently, he had nursed a grudge against David ever since the murder of his granddaughter's husband. Resistance in prayer is the biblical approach to confronting and overcoming the devil. Peter wrote, "Resist him, steadfast in the faith" (1Pet.5:9). James echoed this teaching: "Submit to God. Resist the devil and he will flee from you. Draw near to God and He will draw near to you." (James 4:7-8). Both Peter and James make clear that we are to actively resist evil through our persevering prayers. On the surface,

resistance may appear to be passive, but in practice, it is anything passive. It is an active stance, both intentional and powerful. What would you do if a weight began to press against you, attempting to push you off a position rightfully yours? How would you resist? You will lean into the weight and press back. The pressure you exert would equal or exceed the pressure exerted against you. That is a posture of resistance.

Resistance is a first and foremost a firm decision to join the struggle against evil in prayer, rather than turning away, backing off, or retreating. Such resistance takes strength and courage. It also takes patience and perseverance. That is why Luke includes a parable designed to teach us "that men always ought to pray and not lose heart" (Luke 8:1). Peter and James point to two key words at the heart of our ability to resist the devil through our prayers: Submission to God and faith. Submission to God is saying, "I cannot, but You can. We might say, "Lord, I cannot defeat the devil on my own" in our prayer battlefields, but with You, I can." This is the position apostle Paul took when he said, "I can do all things through Christ who strengthens me" (Phil. 4:13). James taught that submission occurs when we seek to develop closer relationship to God. As we spend time with God, we get to know Him better and discover how He wants us to overcome evil and experience blessing. We draw near to God through prayer and by spending time in His Word. We draw near to God when we set aside time solely to listen to God and to wait upon Him for direction and guidance. We draw near to God when we periodically shut ourselves away, closing off all other influences that might distract us from knowing Him better.

The better we know Him, the more we see His awesome power and His vast love; we learn from His wisdom and experience, and we consequently grow in our faith. We come to an even greater realization: "Yes! God can defeat the devil on my behalf. Yes! God will win in any conflict with the devil. Yes! God does want me to be able to overcome my adversary and to live in victory in Christ Jesus." Faith is saying to God, "I believe you will." In our battle to overcome the enemy, we might pray this way: "I believe You will defeat the enemy and cause him to flee from me as I resist him and put my trust in You." Again, and again, David made this declaration of faith in the Lord: "O my God, I trust in You" (Ps 25:2). We grow in faith by exercising it, by trusting God in situation after situation, circumstances after circumstances, relationship after relationship. We develop a personal history in which we obey God and He remains faithful in His loving care of us. It is impossible for you to resist the devil for very long if you do not believe that Christ Jesus through you can and will defeat the devil. Furthermore, you can remain firm in your faith only when you completely submit to God in all areas of your life. When you do not submit an area to God, you are saying to Him, "I can handle this. I do not need your help." That is precisely the place the devil will attack you!

The good news is that God has given every one of us a measure of faith to develop. He gives us the ability to submit. Therefore, we can resist the devil through our prayers. Afterwards, he must flee.

WHAT DOES IT MEAN TO "PRAY WITHOUT CEASING"?

1Thess. 5:17 "Pray without ceasing" What does the apostle Paul mean by "pray without ceasing"? How is it possible to carry on with normal life while praying without a break? First, the apostle did not mean that we should walk around all day mumbling prayers to God. Rather, he taught that we can live in a constant attitude of prayer, even as we go about our daily routine. Of course, on some days we will pray much more than on others. But regardless of the particular items on our "to do" list for that day, we can maintain a natural attitude of prayer that encompasses our whole lives. When we develop such a prayerful outlook, prayer becomes our first instinct any time we face a challenge or encounter a difficulty. When we maintain an attitude of prayer, we do not have to think about moving from the first gear to second, from an attitude of prayer to the practice of prayer. It never occurs to us that we should not pray.

Should you pray about trivial matters? Yes! God listens to every prayer. Since He is interested in every aspect of your life, He invites you to pray about whatever concerns you, interests you, confuses you, frightens you, or in any way touches or challenges your life. Prayers to find lost glasses or to mentally retrieve forgotten information are both worthy requests. God has called us to be people of prayer. Regular communication on this level creates intimate fellowship with the Savior. Through prayer we discover the goodness and faithfulness of God. But while taking time to get alone with God is the ideal, we do not have to limit ourselves to such times. God hears our prayers no matter where we pray. The devotional writer Oswald Chamber encourages us to put "reckless" confidence in God. He says that too often we limit our praying precisely because we do not cast ourselves on His grace and mercy. Will outsiders consider such wild trust in God foolhardy, even madness? Probably. But so, what? Only through prayer can we tap into the limitless resources of God. Only by praying can we test the Lord's promise: "If you ask anything in My name, I will do it" (John 14:14). Prayer is one of the best ways we have to remind ourselves that God is our gracious Heavenly Father and that we are His much-loved children.

24

HOW CAN I DEVELOP AND MAINTAIN AN ATTITUDE OF ACTIVE LISTENING BEFORE THE LORD?
1KING 19:11-13

MANY PEOPLE SEEM UNCOMFORTABLE WITH SILENCE, especially if they are alone. In silence, however, we are able to hear the "still, small voice" of the Lord. Certainly, the prophet Elijah knew this. After receiving a death threat from Queen Jezebel, Elijah escaped to isolated deserted area. There in a cave, he heard the Lord say to him,

> "Go out and stand on the mountain before the Lord." And behold, the Lord passed by, and a great and strong wind tore into the mountains and broke the rocks in pieces before the Lord, but the Lord was not in the wind; and after the wind

an earthquake, but the Lord was not in the earthquake; and a fire, but the Lord was not in the fire; and the fire a still small voice. So, it was, when Elijah heard it, that he wrapped his face in his mantle and went out and stood in the entrance of the cave. Suddenly a voice came to him, and said, "What are you doing here"

(1 King 19-11-13).

Quietness is essential to listening. If we are too busy to sit in silence in His presence; if we are preoccupied with thoughts or concerns about the day; if have filled our minds for hour upon hour with carnal interference and aimless chatter, then we are going to have difficulty truly listening to the still, small voice of God. Set aside times to "wait upon the Lord" in silence. You may find that late night or early morning is good time for solitude and quietness for you. A noonday walk in the park may be a time when you quiet your soul before the Lord. Ask the Lord to reveal to you a time and place where you might turn off the cares and worries of the world for a few moments and listen to Him. So often we spend our prayer time by talking to the Lord, without spending any time just waiting in silence to see what the Lord might have to say to us. Take time to intentionally sit or knee in silence before the Lord. Empty your mind of all other thoughts. Concentrate on His Word and His presence with you. Ask to speak to you.

LISTENING TO GOD IS ESSENTIAL TO WALKING WITH GOD.

Psalm 81:8 "Hear, O My people, and I will admonish you! O Israel, if you will listen to me! One of the most important lessons we can learn is how to listen to God. In our complex and hectic lives, nothing is more urgent, nothing more necessary and nothing more rewarding than hearing what God has to say to us. A true conversation, of course involves both talking and listening. Most of us do better with the talking part. I used to be so occupied doing the Lord's work that I had no time to pay close attention to God's voice. I went out for evangelism with my two daughters and gave out tracts and bibles to lost souls. Since God had called me to be a worker in His vineyard, I took His service seriously but did not have time to sit still before His presence. I spent time talking to God about my personal needs and the ministry he had put in my hand. I had never spent much time listening to Him. If we do not learn to listen to God, we can make unwise decisions and make very costly mistakes. You may ask, "Does God really speak to us today?" The Bible assures us that He does. The book of Hebrews opens this way: "God who at various times and in various ways spoke in time past to the fathers by the prophets, has in these last days spoken to us by His Son" (Heb. 1:1-2). Our God is not silent. Our Heavenly Father is alive and active.

He speaks to us individually. Furthermore, He does not speak in veiled terms, riddles, or mysteries. He speaks plainly. The goal of any communicator is to be understood, not merely to speak well. God speaks in a way that we can hear Him, receive His message clearly, and understand precisely what He wants us to do. God speaks not only in general and absolute terms, but also to each one of us personally. God is an infinite God, fully capable of communicating with each of us right when we are in the midst of our circumstances in very personal, direct, and explicit terms. This may be the most important concept you will ever grasp in learning how to listen to God when God speaks. Everything in the Bible applies to your life in some way. Every message or communication based on the Word of God carries the truth meant for you. There is nothing in a chapter of the bible, a sermon based on God's Word, or book on God's word, that is not for you. Each of us must take God's Word personally!

God does not play favorites. He does not speak to one child and ignores His other children. His word of correction to you may be personal that you do not want to share it with others, but ultimately, God's word of correction applies to everyone. The same goes for God's promises, provisions, and insights. God does not speak frivolously. He does not joke around. God means what He says and will do what He says. God is serious about His relationship with you. He expects you to respond to His voice, heed His word, and act on it. Listening to God is not casual pastime or a let's -try- it -and- see- if you- like- it activity. Listening to God is the most important thing you can do, for the sake of your eternal soul. So, when you spend time talking to God in prayer, wait silently for Him to see what He has to say. Listen to God's voice, He cares for you!

25

WHAT STEPS CAN I TAKE WHEN I REALLY NEED TO HEAR FROM GOD?
2 KIN 7

THROUGHOUT THE BIBLE, WE READ OF prophets and other men and women God who implored their people to hear the word of the Lord. Obviously, God earnestly wanted His people to hear His voice. He still does. So how do we hear from God when speaks to us today? What steps can we take to make ourselves ready to hear what He has to say? We tend to complicate the process. When we want to ask God what He desires in our lives, we often act as though/=h we would like to receive a phone call from Heaven in which the Lord gives a detailed plan for the next five years. In fact, we already have everything we need in order to discover what He wants for us. Developing daily spiritual disciplines helps us to hear the Lord's voice clearly and seek His direction continually. Ponder the following basic steps you can take to enable you to hear the Lord when He speaks to you: Read God Word by diving every day into

God's Word, we begin to see His established order for our lives. We learn about God's truth, mercy, love, and forgiveness. Seek Him in Prayer. Many times, bowing our head is the best way to see God's face and hear His voice. In opening ourselves up before the Lord, we can honestly discuss our circumstances with Him, listening for His direction as we remain still. Prayer is more than just a wish list for God it is a conversation in which we interact with Him. Meditation; dwelling on what God speaks to our hearts is a great way to let His truths take root in our souls. Not only will what we read or hear from Him impact our lives, but by meditating on it, God has the building material o lay an unshakeable foundation in our hearts. The psalmist said to the Lord, "I have more understanding than all my teachers, for Your testimonies are my meditation" (Ps. 119:99). You hear with your ears. if you have normal hearing you can't help hearing sounds within a certain audio range. Listening, however, goes further, involving the mind. Genuine listening is active, meaning that it puts the mind in gear and hears everything said, looking intently for the meaning. That's how God wants us to listen to Him actively!

PRAYER IS LIFE'S GREATEST TIME SAVER

When my family moved to New York, I couldn't seem to find the right job. It took me more than a year before I was employed in a place that I felt good about. I got support from my church and a family friend before getting the job. As you can imagine, I desired for my own job and was asking God for it, but I could not get it. I could not understand what God was up to by not immediately meeting my desire. During the period of waiting I asked, 'Why did

God not answer my prayer on time? I asked. But God was watching over me and He eventually answered my prayer when he felt I had been well equipped to go out to work. Prayer not only spares us a lot of trouble; it saves us a lot of time. God's answer seems like a delay to us, but in fact it keeps us from wasting countless hours trying to search for something He had not call us to do. Prayer is life's greatest time saver. Jesus spoke of this relationship between an apparent delay in God's answers to our prayers, and the fact of how it saves us time. In Luke 18 He told a parable to teach us "that men always ought to pray and not lose heart" (V.1). That doesn't sound like a passage on how prayer saves time, does it? Yet by the end of His story, Jesus explained His point like this: "And shall God not avenge His own elect who cry out day and night to Him, though He bears long with them? I tell you that He will avenge them speedily" (Luke 18:7,8). Did you catch it, God may "bear long" with us in our prayers, and yet He is committed to acting on our behalf "speedily." That means that prayer really is life's greatest time saver, for God will answer our prayers as soon as it is best for us not one moment sooner, not one second later. What may feel like a delay to us is actually God sparing us tremendous amounts of wasted time. One of the church's television broadcasts was taken off the air because of the conflict within the church. After the church resolved the conflict, the church asked the same station if they could be rescheduled at their station prior broadcast time, the request was refused. The church also offered to buy time on the station, but the request was as well refused. The church believe God wanted them on television, so they prayed that He would once again allow them to begin a television ministry. When the members of the church started praying, they thought something would open up soon. But it took them a year before they got results. Eventually two stations offered them a spot in their weekly programming. One opportunity led to another, till today their service is broadcast through "In Touch Ministries" throughout the world. God did not answer their prayer to be put back on the air for a season. He waited and provided church with something much better than was asked for.

Many young people pray and pray that the Lord will send provide them with marriage partners. As they enter their late twenties, many of them challenge God's interest. They wonder, "What is God waiting for?" God may be waiting for the time He knows they are ready. What seems like a delay to them is actually sparing them countless hours, days, months, even years of heartache. As I reflect on my life, I realize that if God had answered certain prayers of mine according to my own timing, I would have missed His best in every case. Imagine for a moment what a five-year-old would do with a pocketknife and a flashlight. A good father might not mind giving the knife to him, but the boy needs to grow up before he can be trusted with it. In the same way, God waits for us to grow spiritually in some areas before He gives us all the spiritual and material blessings, He has in store for us (Eph. 1:3). God will answer our prayers sooner or one second later. This is why prayer really is life's greatest time saver.

26

HOW CAN I ENRICH MY TIME ALONE WITH GOD?

HAVE YOU EVER SAT DOWN IN a quiet place with your Bible, ready to have a devotional time with the Lord but you felt aimless? Maybe you flipped through the pages and finally settled on a psalm. But then you remembered another appointment, so you said a quick prayer and told yourself you would pray more later but it never happened. You are not alone if you feel frustrated with the quality of your quiet times. As much as you may desire real intimacy with your personal Savior, however, remember that He longs for it even more. James 4:8 promises, "Draw near to God and He will draw near to you." It helps many people to get some direction on how to develop a close walk with Christ. Specific goals can help you to focus on His Word daily. First select a plan that fits your understanding. Remember, spending time with God will almost never just "fit in" to your daily routine. You must schedule and then jealously guard your time with God. The more you honor that appointment the greater your enrichment. Have you run across puzzling words or passages? Instead of waiting until later to consider the issues, sit down with a Bible dictionary and concordance or other study aids. You may resolve your question completely but seeking His truth on your own can spur amazing growth.

Maybe you cannot afford to purchase your own Bible study tools. Never give up! Seek other options. A lot of good Bible reference materials are available free on internet. Some churches have libraries where you can borrow what you need, as do selected public libraries. Ask your pastor or church associate if they have materials you may use. Most people find the body of Christ eager to help in this pursuit. As you read the Bible have a notebook and pen ready to write a spiritual journal. Some people record their daily prayers, leaving a space to describe how God answered them. You may prefer a format in which you write down a special verse and describe why it impacted you. If you have a journal before, you know what a treat it is to see a reminder of your spiritual journey. Are you ready for a relationship with Jesus that knows no boundaries? Then open your time, your life, your heart and expect the Lord's involvement.

MEETING A FEARSOME GOD

Thunder and lighting, a thick cloud, smoke loud trumpeting and then the voice of God, were all experienced by Israelites when God descends to the top of the Mount Sinai (Ex19:16-19). They tremble "with fear" (Ex 20:18)- imagine the crying and the chaos as mothers call for their children and as families gather together. They cower in God's fearsome presence, expecting death. Have you experienced the immensity of God's power, majesty and holiness? Few people have and few people want to. It is much more pleasant to think about the beautiful, peaceful, loving face of God than his mightiness, holiness and power. Does God want us to be afraid of Him? What distinction does Moses make between being afraid of God and fearing God (Ex 20:20)? If fearing God is not the same as being afraid of God, what does it mean to fear God (Heb 12:18-29)? What are the benefits of fearing God (Ps. 25:14; 31:19; Pr 14:26-27)? What are the consequences of not fearing God (Jer. 5:21-25)? The Israelites put their trust in other gods, in human strength, in power and in wealth. Have you put your trust in something or someone other than God? To fear God is to acknowledge his holiness and power, to respect and honor him and to stand in awe of Him. Those who rebel against God should be afraid of Him. Their rebellion incurs his anger (Ps. 90:7:11). But if you are His child, God does not want you to be afraid of Him.

Exodus 3:1-6. Moses' first encounter with God terrifies him. However, as their relationship becomes more intimate, God speaks to Moses "face to face as a man speaks with his friend" (Exodus 33:11). Later Moses boldly asks God, "show me your glory" (Exodus 33:18). God then come down in the cloud and stands there with Moses proclaiming that He is "the Lord, the compassionate and gracious God, slow to anger, abounding in love and faithfulness, maintaining love to thousands, and forgiving wickedness (Exodus 34:5-7) As Moses comes to know God more and more intimately, he is less afraid than more fearful that he is, he was awed by God's holiness. Are you afraid of God? Or do you fear him? God desires an intimate relationship with you. If you want to see His face, you can be certain that one day your desire will be realized (Rev. 22: 4).

The Israelites prepare themselves for meeting God by consecrating themselves and washing their clothes (Ex 19:10). Purity is a necessity in the presence of a Holy God. You are made pure through Jesus' blood (Heb13:11-12; 1Jn. 1:7). He is your righteousness (1

Co 1:30). Use the Scripture (such as Psalm 99:1-5) to express your adoration to God. Write your own psalm of praise, or sing a song to God, he will draw near to you (Jas 4:8). The time you spend with him is time like no other because he is like no other (Jer. 10:6-7). If you are afraid, ask God to show himself to you as your loving and compassionate friend. The Holy Spirit will be your helper as you yield to God, learn to trust him and begin to enjoy his presence.

27

HOW CAN I PARTNER WITH THE HOLY SPIRIT IN MY LIFE?

BEFORE I ANSWER, LET ME ASK a question. What allowed you to begin a relationship with God? How did you a sinner enter a friendship with a Holy God? What brought the two of you together? Was it dedication on your part? Was it a result of your unceasing effort? Of course not! You entered it by faith. And nothing has changed. "As you therefore have received Christ Jesus the Lord, so walk in Him, rooted and built up in Him and established in the faith, as you have been taught" (Col. 2:6,7). We are not the first generation of Christians who have tried to take matters into our own hands; the early church had the same problem. It is part of fallen human nature to want to maintain control, to do things ourselves. When it comes to righteousness, whether for salvation or for living, we must allow God to do the work. The Spirit-filled life is a life of faith. It started by faith, and it runs on faith. It is faith from start to finish. Then we believed that Jesus saved us from the power of sins; now we must believe that He saves us from the power of sin. Then we trusted Him for forgiveness, and it became ours; now we must trust Him for righteousness, and it shall become ours also. Then we took Him as a Savior from the penalties for our sins; now We must take Him as a Savior from the bondage of our sins. Then He will be lifted out of the pit; He will seat us in Heavenly places with Himself. The Bible never makes a distinction between the faith that saved us from the penalty of sin, once and for all, and the faith that saves us from the power of sin, every day. It is all the same. So, what is faith? Faith is believing that God will do as He has promised. Faith is not a power or something we are supposed to drum up inside ourselves. Faith is trusting that God will honor His promises. That is all there is to it. We are to go about our lives, making decisions, handling crises, raising our families, and so on, as if God will really do what He said He would do. That is what it means to partner with the Spirit.

TRUSTING GOD MEANS LOOKING BEYOND WHAT WE CAN SEE TO WHAT GOD SEES

Starring across the Leah Valley into the eyes of Goliath, David recalled the times God had delivered him from the brink of disaster. God had always given him the ability he needed to triumph. Now he faced one of the greatest challenges of his life -a trained and well-armed warrior named Goliath. At some point, each of us will face what will look like mammoth trials and difficulties. That is why we must know how to respond to every threat by laying hold of the kind of victorious faith that looks beyond what we can see so what God sees. The secret of David's success was his ability to trust and obey God. Had he looked merely at the giant challenge facing him, he would have turned around and run away, as did the rest of the Israelites. But through faith, David saw what his countrymen did not. In times of extreme pressure, God stretches our faith and deepens our dependence on Him. Without a strong abiding faith, we can quickly yield to temptation and fear, especially when the trial or difficulty is intense or prolonged. God developed David's trust until it became unshakeable. Whatever Goliath you face, you need to bury one truth deep within your heart: God loves you, and when you place your trust in Him, He will not allow you to suffer defeat. You may go through times of failure. Life may not always turn out the way you planned but ultimately, God will be glorified, and you will be blessed. Every challenge presents an opportunity for God to display His faithfulness and love. Instead of yielding to thoughts of fear and failure, make a commitment to trust God, even when you do not know what the next day will bring. Train yourself to look beyond what you can see to what God sees.

David founded his faith in the sovereignty of God; that is why he knew he would not fail in his quest to defeat the Philistine giant. How can you gain that kind of faith? David recalled how God had delivered him from the paw of lion and the grasp of the bear (1 Samuel 17:32-37). You first win spiritual victories in your mind. If you cave into feelings of fear and doubt, you will lose. When you focus on the truth of God's Word, you win every time. No one in the Israelite camp encouraged David in his quest to defeat Goliath. The soldiers laughed at him. His brother felt embarrassed by his presence and urged him to go home. Even King Saul doubted David. If he had listened to their disparaging comments, he would have given up but he turned his heart toward God and there found the encouragement he needed. David entered the battle shouting to his arrogant opponent the memorable words, "the battle is the Lord's and He will give you into our hands" (1 Samuel 17:47). What a victorious way to say, "God win!" You can face any circumstances with confidence and hope, because it is not you strengthen, wisdom, energy or power that brings victory. Triumph comes because of God's ability, and when you place your trust in Him, you tap into an irresistible force that no one and nothing can successfully oppose.

28

INTIMACY WITH GOD

THE SPIRIT OF GOD OFTEN SPEAKS to us in the stillness of our hearts with a word of conviction or assurance. When the Holy Spirit is directing us away from something harmful, we very often have a heaviness or a feeling of trouble, foreboding of uneasiness in our spirits. When Holy Spirit is directing us toward helpful things, we tend to feel a deep inner peace, an eagerness to see what God will do, and a feeling of joy. The Holy Spirit has come to reveal the truth to us. He has come in His all-knowing ability to impart to us what we need to know in order to live obedient and faithful lives. Trust Him to guide you, now and always!

Does the idea of intimacy with God frighten you? "Who could be intimate with a Holy, Righteous God?" You ask. Yes, God is holy and righteous, and he is also loving and compassionate. God reveals himself in Scripture as a father and as a husband. He provides for you and protects you as loving father. As your husband he desires to meet your need for intimacy. The most intimate human experience is the relationship between a husband and a wife. The Bible reveals God's desire for that type of intimacy through allegories like that in the book of Hosea and through individual passages like Isaiah 54:5:

"For your maker is your husband, the Lord Almighty is His name." Today, Bible scholars emphasize the need to take Song of Songs at face value as clear and unapologetic love poetry, but historically this book has been viewed as God comparing intimacy with his people to the all-consuming adoration between two lovers. Song of Songs 2:1-3 expresses the delight lovers find in each other. Who does God delight in (Ps 147:11)? What does God give to those who delight in him (Ps37:4). The lover sees the beloved as unique as and more desirable than others (SS 2:2). How does God see you (Eph 1:4-6; 1Pe2 2:9)? The lover proclaims to all that the beloved is his and he loves her (SS 2:5-6). How does God proclaim His love for you (Eph 1:7-14)?

The beloved finds strength, refreshment, and tenderness in her lover (SS 2:8-9). What needs do you have that Jesus can supply? The beloved longs for her lover's presence and rejoice when he is near (SS 2:8-9). Do you long for God's presence? (Ps 16:11; 1 Jn. 3:19-20). What can you experience long for Go's presence? The lover calls to the beloved, drawing her with promises of love and fulfillment (SS 2:10-13). What is the beloved's warning (SS 2:7)? Love for God cannot be feigned or invented. When your love for God and your desire to be in His presence become a hunger and longing, you are approaching the depth of intimacy that God desires to have with you. God is in pursuit of you, and He wants an intimate relationship with you one that we last forever, one that will satisfy your deepest needs. You can respond to God by allowing him to draw you into his loving arms. Your life, your relationships, your reactions all will be affected by God's embrace. If you desire intimacy with God, go to Him in prayer, He is waiting. He will rejoice, and He will treat you with tenderness and compassion (Isa 40:11). He is the perfect lover of your soul, one who will never disappoint (Roman 5:5), one who will be faithful, true and loving (Ps 145:13; Rev 19:11). How long before you say, "My lover is mine and I am His" (SS 2:16)?

29

GOD'S PURSUIT OF YOU

EACH DAY IN THE GARDEN OF Eden is perfect. The soft ground cushions Adam and Eve's bare feet. The dew waters their surroundings to perfect, lush green. Evenings in the garden are even better if perfection can be improved on. That is when Adam and Eve walk with God, His presence surpasses the rest of their day and brings them joy and peace. But this day is different. They hear the "sound of the Lord God" as He walks "in the garden in the cool of the day" (Gen 3:8). But they do not run to meet Him. They do not feel the way they used to. They hide because they are filled with shame, a new emotion for them. God is calling you too. Are you running to meet Him or are you hiding from Him? Shame can prevent an intimate, personal relationship with God. But it is important to differentiate between true shame and false shame. You feel true shame if you feel guilty of your sin (and all of us sin). You feel false shame if you feel dirty because another person sinned against you (for example, the shame felt by victims of sexual or spousal abuse or rape). If you have been wounded by someone else's sin, you may feel a sense of shame, but it is not true shame. Bring true shame to the cross of

Jesus for forgiveness. Bring false shame into the arms of Jesus for healing (1 Peter 2:24). Adam and Eve feel shame. What is the root of their shame and guilt (Gen 3:11)? What have you done that causes you to feel shame? What is the root of your shame (Roman 3:10-12)? Adam and Eve cover their nakedness (the outward evidence of their shame) with a few flimsy fig leaves. What have you done to try to cover your shame? Have your efforts had any impact? (Isa 59:2). What has Jesus done to remove your shame and where do you stand with God now? If your sin seems so great or horrible to be forgiven or if your shame seems so overwhelming that it can't be removed, remember, Jesus loves you so much that he has already taken your sin and shame on himself. He makes you clean from it. Receive his gift and let him wash your shame away. Despite your past no matter what you have done God loves you with an everlasting love; "I have drawn you with loving-kindness" (Jer. 31:3). If your shame is for your own sin, write the name of that sin on a sheet of paper. Then with a pencil write the word shame in a large letter across the paper. Jesus knows what has happened, and He loves you anyway. In prayer, confess your sin and your need for Jesus. In faith, erase the word shame. Now write in ink the word forgiven across your paper. Remember: "Those who look to him are radiant; their faces are never covered with shame" (Ps 34:5).

BROKEN RELATIONSHIPS

One of the saddest chapters in the bible, 1 Samuel 15 tells of disobedience, greed, lies, denial and shifting blame. The outcome: broken relationships with people and with God. How does Saul go from being God's chosen king to being rejected by God? Well, it certainly did not happen overnight, and rejecting Saul was not a snap decision on God's part. Here is a portrait of a man who is more like us than we care to admit. What command does God give to Saul in 1 Samuel15:3? To "totally destroy" seems abhorrent to us today. But God used total destruction to punish nations for their sin and to preserve them from vile influences. How does Saul disobey this command (Isa 15:8-9)? How does offering to God (through death) the "despised and weak" animals show disrespect for God (Mal 1:7-12)? How does keeping the best animals for themselves show greed (1 Sa. 15:9, 19)? What are some ways you have saved the best for yourself? How does Saul reveal his pride? (1 Sa? 5:12). Saul takes the credit for what is done right, and he blames others for what is done wrong. Do you ever play the shifting blame game? How does this interfere with your relationship with God? What is Saul's punishment? How does this go beyond the punishment he had previously received for disobedience? What does this reveal about God (Joel 2:13)? What does Saul's unconscious use of the pronoun "your" (1Samuel 15:15, 21, 30) say about this relationship with God? How does he try to keep up outward appearance of having a relationship with God? Have you ever done this when and why? How does Saul reveal that his repentance is not heartfelt but simply an attempt to escape judgment? When have you made excuses for your sin when God required true repentance? How does this prevent reconciliation with God? If you are unfamiliar with the story of David and Bathsheba you may want to read 2 Samuel 11. David committed adultery with Bathsheba and then had Bathsheba's husband, Uriah killed to cover up what he had done. Nathan the prophet confronts David with his sin. Although David's confession is the same as Saul's "I have sinned" (1 Samuel15:24; 2 Samuel 12:13). David's attitude is totally different. He responds with true repentance and is immediately forgiven (2 Samuel 12:13). True repentance is more than a simple "you are right; True repentance is immediately forgiven (2Sa 12:13). True repentance is more than a simple "you are right; I am sorry," True repentance is a heartfelt recognition of guilt, accompanied by a desire for restoration and a turning away from sin. God forgives David's sin and David devotes himself to the Lord all the rest of his life. He is remembered as one who "had done what was right in the eyes of the Lord and had not failed to keep any of the Lord's commands all the days of his life, except in the case of Uriah the Hittite" (1King 15:5).

Are you alienated from God because of sin and disobedience? Return to Him. He will not turn away from a broken and contrite heart (Ps 51:17). Your broken relationship can be restored only if your heart is broken in repentance. Bring the pieces of your heart and your life to Jesus, the only One who can mend them.

30

THE VOICE OF GOD

IMAGINE HEARING THE VOICE OF GOD! Moses seems to accept this as a normal occurrence. And in fact, it is normal for Moses. The words "the Lord said to Moses" appear 138 times in the Old Testament, the words "the Lord said," 290 times. God was not silent then, and he is not silent today. Even though he might not speak audibly, God still has much to say to us. Has the Lord ever spoken to you (see John 14:26; 1Jn 2:27)? What are some ways the Holy Spirit might communicate with you? And how do you know if the voice is God's? The Bible is the Chief way the Spirit speaks and is the test for all the other voices that claim to be God's. it is "living and active". (Heb 4:12). It tells us who God is and who we are. What particular insight has it given you lately about God or about yourself? The Holy Spirit sometimes spoke directly to Paul; however, other times he used people to guide Paul (Act 21:10-11). Has God ever seemed to use someone to guide you? Describe what happened. As you look back, do you think the guidance passes the test of agreement with the scripture? Why or why not? The Spirit sometimes speaks through visions and dreams. Peter learned an important lesson through a vision (Act 10:9-10). Have you ever had a dream or a vision that you felt was from God? What was the dream or vision like? What did He reveal to you? As you look back do you think the dream or vision passes the test of agreeing with the scripture? Why or why not? The Holy Spirit sometimes uses circumstances to communicate with people. God used Esther's circumstances to save his people. When have you felt that God used your circumstances to speak with you? Looking back, do you think your interpretation of the circumstances agrees with Scripture's teaching? Why or why not. The Spirit can put thought in people's minds. He put the plans for the temple into David's mind (1Chronicles 28:12, 19). Have you ever had plans, ideas, or mental impressions that you felt were from God? Describe them. As you look back on them, do you think your ideas were in keeping with Scripture? Why or why not? God is a person; He wants to have a relationship with you. In others, relationship requires communication. In other words, He may be speaking, but are you listening? And if you are listening, are you testing the voice of God to see if it is God's? Jeremiah 32:6-9. Jeremiah receives word from God telling him to buy a field. He does not act immediately. Perhaps he is not sure the message is from God. Only when his cousin comes to him and says, "buy my field," that Jeremiah became certain the message comes from God. What should you do if you think you hear God speaking, but you are not sure? Try to test a mental impression to see if it is from the Lord (1Jn 4-1-3). A word from God will always agree with the Bible. He will not contradict himself. A word from God will also be consistent with Christ's character. If you are a believer in Christ, you have the Holy Spirit in you, and you should sense agreement with a message that's truly from God. Ask yourself: Am I fixing my spiritual eyes on Jesus or have my own wishes tainted the impression? Am I obeying Scripture, or am I being deceived? During your prayer time, listen for the Lord to speak to your heart, perhaps through a Bible verse, a song, a mental impression or a reaction of some kind. You may sense a response in yourself of faith, awe, peace, praise and healing. The Spirit speaks to the core of your being, filling that deep place in you that place no one else can reach.

THE SINGING GOD

Imagine hearing God sing. Does it sound like the mighty roar of thunder (Joel 3:16), or like a soft and gentle whisper (1King 19:12)? It is powerful and strong, yet unimaginably beautiful, pure and sweet. And he is singing that glorious song over you! Why does God sing over you? Because he delights in you. You make his heart sing with joy. Do you believe this? If not, why not? There are obstacles; you say your sin and guilt, your constant wandering from God, the enemy's accusations that you are unworthy, and your fear of rejection. Let's look at each of these obstacles so you can grasp the fact that all you need you already possess. God's mercy, grace, love and presence are already yours. Yes, you are a sinner. That is the very reason for you to go to Him. What has God done for you and why did He do it. (1Ti 1:5; Tit 3:4-7)? God is delighted when you obey (Dt. 30:9-10). If you wander from Him, He will discipline you (Pr 3:11-12; Heb 12:5-11). What is God's goal in discipline (2 Co 7:9-10)? How does God quiet your feelings for rejection and unworthiness (Zep? 3:17)? It is not His power or His majesty that quieten your fears; it is his unfailing love (Ps. 36:7-8; Isa 54:10). What is God's promise to you (Jer. 32:38)? Do you believe this? God rejoices when he can do good things for you (Ps 32:41)? He delights in your well-being (Ps35:27). What about your enemy, the accuser

(Isa 50:7-9; 54:16-17; Zep. 3:15)? Why will God never reject you (1Sa 12:22; Ps 94-14)? God's name is glorified when he pours out love and good on His people. For His own name's sake, His glory will never forsake you (Isa 48:9-11). God's love for you is deep and strong. It will never be shaken. You are secure in Him. Knowing that He delights in you can give you freedom to delight in Him and in all that He has for you.

Ezekiel 36:24-32 is the beautiful passage that is meaningful every believer. God rejoices over you and desires to bless you with these things: freedom, cleansing, a new not remodeled heart and spirit, His very own Spirit within you to enable you to obey, personal relationship with him and prosperity (Eze. 36:28-30). God will remove your impurities, your heart of stone, your uncleanness and your disgrace. In all of this God's holy name is glorified. Your transportation brings him glory. You are an example of His grace, mercy, love and power! He is your loving Father. Listen to the special love song he is singing just for you.

AN EXPERIENCE OF GOD

This passage is Paul's attempt to describe what many believe to have been his own experience or encounter with God. Paul relates an experience that happened 14 years before but that had not lost its mystery or its influence on his life. Some people today are uncomfortable talking about such experiences, while others spend their lives desiring them. What can you learn from this Biblical description of an actual experience with God? What does Paul call this experience and from whom did it originate (2 Cor. 12:1)? Paul's experience makes such an impression on him that 14 years later he has not forgotten it. Is it a spiritual experience or is his body involved? Does it really seem to matter? To What place is Paul "caught up" (2Cor 12:2)? The "Third Heaven" is beyond the earth's atmosphere, beyond outer space as humans know it and into God's presence. What do you think "caught up" means? Without comparing type or degree, describe an experience you had in which you felt your spirit was somehow lifted up a time of deep communion with God in which you experienced something beyond yourself? Did it seem too holy to share with others? Why or why not? What things does Paul hear (2 Cor. 12:4)? Paul's experience with God is meant for Paul and God's alone. How do you think this experience strengthened Paul's relationship with God? What role should an experience can strengthen a person's relationship with God? What role should an experience with God play in the foundation of your faith? An intimate relationship with God often brings with an experience one that is mysterious because God himself is mysterious. In Isaiah 6:1-7, Isaiah reports on an encounter with God that takes place either in the body or out of the body. We are not told if the experience is spiritual (a vision) or physical (material, in the body). It doesn't seem matter. What matters is that the experience is real. Isaiah's response to his encounter with God is dread seeing God's holiness only amplifies Isaiah's perception of his own sin and unworthiness. But God provides a way for Isaiah to reach God. After a seraph touches a hot coal to Isaiah's lips, God tells him, "You guilt is taken away and sin atoned for" (Isa 6:7). God desires encounters with his children. He has given his own Son so that he can have an encounter with you. Isaiah's encounter with the Holy One changes him forever. Have you had such an encounter? How has it changed you? Through Jesus, God has provided the way to intimacy with him. Your experience of God may not be as "inexperience" as Paul, but it can be just as real and just as life changing. God's purpose in offering his only Son for your sin is to reconcile you to himself (Roman 5:10). His intent is to have intimate relationship with you. Go to him in prayer. Permit him to love you. Permit yourself to have a mysterious encounter with him. The type or degree of your experience is unimportant. What is important is that you encounter him.

31

GOD'S LOVE AND MERCY

THE HEBREW AND GREEK WORDS FOR mercy are often translated "love" or "compassion." The words convey a concern that moves a person to help. It is more than a feeling; it is feeling that prompts action an action that is underserved by the one who benefits from it. In this passage, the prophet Joel characterized God as "compassionate and abounding in love" How is God described in psalm 103:3-8-14? When do you confuse the attributes of your Heavenly Father with those of your earthly father, thinking that God will respond to you as your earthly father has? Psalm 78 lists some of the many things the Israelites do to deserve God's wrath. How does God respond? Their rebellion brings God's discipline, but God's judgment is mixed with mercy. When have you experienced God's disciplines those he loves (Rev 3:19), his mercy outlives his anger (Ps 103:10-11)? Do you ever fear rejection from God? If you return to him, how will he respond? God is holy and righteous. That causes fear. But Jesus had paid the debt incurred by your sin (Rom 5:8-9). He has saved you from God's wrath. Even your salvation is accomplished because of God's mercy. And he delights to show you his mercy. Have you ever wondered what you would do if you were in the same shoes of the unmerciful servant? This servant was forgiven a huge debt, one he could never hope to repay. Yet despite the mercy shown to him by his master, he refused to forgive another servant of a debt that amounted to a pittance. How will you respond to those who need mercy from you? God requires that you extend justice, mercy and compassion to others. When Jesus walked on earth, he reminded his listeners that the important matters of the law are justice, mercy and faithfulness (Mt 23:23). The opposite of mercy is judgment. When you are judgmental or refuse to show mercy, as the servant does in this parable, you will face judgment because "judgment without mercy will be shown to anyone who has not been merciful" (Jas 2:13). When you realized the extent of God's mercy toward you, your heart will overflow with love and gratitude. The greater the debt canceled, the greater the love and gratitude in response. If you are having trouble forgiving others or being merciful, perhaps you have yet to discover the depth of God's mercy toward you. Are you the rebellious child needing to return to your Father? Are you the unmerciful servant denying others they need so much? "Have mercy on me, O God, according to your unfailing love, according to your great compassion blot out my transgression" (Ps 51:1). Rebellion an, unrepentant heart of disobedience will keep you from feeling the love and mercy of God. Rend your heart and not your garments. Return to the Lord your God, for he is gracious and compassionate" (Joel 2:13).

GOD'S LOVE FOR THE WANDERER

Israel, God' chosen people wander so far and their unfaithfulness is so blatant that God compares them to "adulterers, burning like an oven" who "love" the wages of a prostitute" (Hos. 9:1) That is harsh! In Hosea 11, Israel is compared to a wayward son who is loved by his father in spite of everything. You can probably see a little of Israel in yourself (Isa 53:6). "We all, like sheep, have gone astray, each of us has turned to our own way; and the LORD has laid on him the iniquity of us all." What is God's response to your wandering? What will your response to him be? Describe God's attitude toward "young" Israel. "When Israel was a child, I loved him, and out of Egypt I called my son." (Hos. 11:1). What has God's attitude been toward you since before time began (Eph 1:4-6)? Where was Israel when God called (Hos. 11:1)? Where were you when God called you? Israel does not realize how God constantly has led her, cared for her and lifted her burdens. As you think back on your life, how has God faithfully "led you with cords of human kindness, with ties of love" (Hos. 11:4)? If you are wandering from God, return to him through repentance (Hos.14:1-2). He will receive you with open arms, will draw you to himself and will rejoice. God's compassion and love are far greater than your sins. (Ps. 103:8-14). He is saying even now, "I have swept away your offenses like a cloud, your sins like the morning mist. Return to me, for I have redeemed you" (Isaiah 44:22). Jesus sees wandering sheep as a priority (Lk.19:10). "For the Son of Man came to seek and to save the lost." Do you know a wandering sheep? Are you one yourself? Jesus will never throw up his hands in frustration and leave you to your own device. He will come running to find you. "He tends his flock like a shepherd: He gathers the lambs in his arms and carries them close to his heart; he gently leads those that have young" (Isa 40:11). This is your Savior, your shepherd your friend.

32

AN EAGER ANTICIPATION OF THE LORD'S RETURN KEEPS US LIVING PRODUCTIVELY

"And Behold I am coming quickly, and My reward is with Me, to give everyone according to his work." (Rev 22:12). Throughout Scripture we find three admonitions given to us about the Lord's return: Watch faithfully, work diligently and wait peacefully. The Lord said repeatedly that we are to watch for His coming because we do not know the day or hour of his return (Matt. 24:42; 25:13). In Luke 21:36) Jesus gave this specific instruction: Watch, therefore, and pray always that you may be counted worthy to escape all these things that will come to pass, and to stand before the Son of Man." We are to do more than pray as we watch. We are to stand fast in faith, with courage and strength (1Cor.16:13). We are to watch soberly arming ourselves with faith and love and salvation (1Thess.5:8). As we watch, we are to remain especially aware of false prophets; we are to discern the spirits and to reject soundly all who do not confess that Jesus Christ is God in the flesh (1John 4:1-2; 2 Peter 2:1). Jesus spoke to John in vision and gave this great promise to those who remain watchful: "Behold, I am coming as a thief. Blessed is he who watches." (Rev. 16:15). Why does Jesus leave us here on earth after He saves us? Why aren't we born again and then immediately taken into the Lord's presence? Because we still have work to do? First, God calls us to win souls. We are to be the Lord's witnesses telling of the love of God and the atoning death of Jesus Christ for sin. We are to testify about what He has done in our lives, both with our own lives, both with our words and by our examples. So long as there remains a soul on earth who hasn't heard the gospel of our Lord Jesus Christ, we have work to do! Second, we are to grow spiritually, developing an ever-increasing intimacy with the Lord. None of us fully lives up to our spiritual potential. We all have room to grow. In those areas where we discover we are unlike Christ, we must work with the Spirit to become conformed to His likeness. Our minds must be renewed (Roman 12:1). Our inner hurts and emotions must be healed. We must grow in spiritual discernment and in the wisdom of God. Our faith must be strengthened and used so that our prayers and our actions more effectively build up the Lord's Kingdom. Waiting is not easy. Impatience often leads to frustration. Waiting can also cause a buildup of fear; the longer something anticipated does not happen, the greater our concern with what will happen, which can degenerate into worry over what coming might happen and fear is only a step away. The Angels spoke peace to the earth at Jesus' first coming (Luke 2:14). More than four hundred times in the Scriptures, the Lord says that we are not to fear, but to enjoy peace. The prophet Isaiah referred to Jesus as the Prince of Peace (Is. 9:6). Throughout His ministry, the Lord Jesus spoke peace: to the woman with an issue of blood He said, "Go in peace"; to a stormy sea He said, "Peace be still; and to His disciples He said, "My peace I give you." The Lord calls us to peace as we await His return. Apart from Jesus, there is no peace not within a human heart, and not among human beings or nations. With Jesus, we can experience peace that passes our rational minds and settles deep within (Phil 4:7). We are to seek and find this peace as we await the Lord's return. When the Lord comes, will He find you among those who love Him and call Him Savior and Lord? When the Lord comes, will He find you doing what He has command you to do? When the Lord comes, will He find you eager to see Him? When the Lord comes, will He find you ready for His appearing? When the Lord calls with a shout from Heaven will you instantly rise to be with Him? When the Lord appears in the clouds, will your heart rejoice with exceedingly great joy? You have it within your grasp to positively answer these questions. How will you choose to respond to the Lord's challenges upon your life? The fact is: He is coming again? Please give your life to Him! Tomorrow might be too late. If you have read this book and you believe in your heart that Jesus died for your sin pray this prayer on the next page.

HEAVENLY FATHER,

I COME IN THE NAME OF JESUS CHRIST. I BELIEVE IN MY HEART THAT JESUS CHRIST IS THE SON OF GOD. I BELIEVE IN MY HEART THAT HE DIED FOR MY SINS; I BELIEVE THAT YOU RAISE HIM FROM THE DEAD FOR MY JUSTIFICATION. I RECEIVE HIM TODAY AS MY PERSONAL LORD AND SAVIOUR AND I GIVE GOD THE GLORY.

AMEN

When you pray this prayer, the peace of God will reign in your life. You also will begin to experience the God's presence in your life. You become one of His children the moment you give your life to Him. It might be too late. Give your life to Jesus today! Hurry up! Jesus is coming soon. Do you want to have an encounter with Jesus? Your answer might be yes! If I can have an encounter with Jesus, you too can do the same. Jesus loves you!

BIBLIOGRAPHY

Sarah Young (2011). "Jesus Calling Devotional Bible" *Holy Bible, New King James Version*. Thomas Nelson 1982.